Roland Allen: Pioneer of Spontaneous Expansion

J.D. Payne

Roland Allen: Pioneer of Spontaneous Expansion
ISBN: 978-1475123890

Published in 2012 by J. D. Payne

Cover photo: 3d Network Connections, Hemera, Thinkstock.
Cover design: Amber Walsh

Other books by J. D. Payne

Missional House Churches: Reaching Our Communities with the Gospel

The Barnabas Factors: Eight Essential Practices for Church Planting Team Members

Discovering Church Planting: An Introduction to the Whats, Whys, and Hows of Global Church Planting

Evangelism: A Biblical Response to Today's Questions

Strangers Next Door: Immigration, Migration, and Mission

Kingdom Expressions: Trends Influencing the Advancement of the Gospel

To Him alone Who is able to bring about
the spontaneous expansion of the Church

Table of Contents

Preface

I was first introduced to Roland Allen as a seminary student. I had heard about his thoughts regarding missions, but had yet to read them for myself. It was during my studies that I was introduced to *Missionary Methods: St. Paul's or Ours?* and quickly found myself wanting to know more about the author and his other writings. I did not know that a major portion of my doctoral dissertation would be devoted to the study of Roland Allen, requiring me to read most of what he wrote and what others wrote about him.

Someone once asked me about the most influential books on my life and ministry—other than the Bible. Without needing to give much thought to my answer, I said that *Missionary Methods* easily made the list. I have also discovered that many other pastors, missionaries, and missiologists who consumed this book were forever changed.

Once a person decides to walk the path with Roland Allen, he or she will likely experience a growing restlessness against the status quo. Gone will be the days when ministry and missions are approached with a lackadaisical attitude. The hunger for gospel advancement may take the place of business-as-usual.

But a warning must be extended to the sojourner who enters into Allen's world. The reader will quickly realize that in order to overcome any unhealthy realities that hinder the multiplication of disciples, leaders, and churches, sacrifice is required. Sometimes great sacrifice.

Lesslie Newbigin was aware of the risks involved when reading these writings. In his Foreword to the American edition of *Missionary Methods,* he penned these words:

> I have thought it right to enter these two words of caution, because the reader should be warned that he is embarking on a serious undertaking. Once he has started reading Allen, he will be compelled to go on. He will find that this quiet voice has a strange relevance and immediacy to the problems of the Church in our day. And I shall be surprised if he does not find before long that any of his accustomed ideas are being questioned by a voice more searching than the word of man.[1]

This year marks the 100th anniversary of the publication of Roland Allen's book *Missionary Methods: St. Paul's or Ours?* It is in recognition of this historic event that I have published this book. It is my hope that *Roland Allen: Pioneer of Spontaneous Expansion* will help you develop a better appreciation of Allen's life and work. I hope you will be inspired to return to his writings and read them for yourself. But above all else, I pray this brief book will bring glory to the Lord as we learn from Allen when it comes to the multiplication of disciples, leaders, and churches throughout the world.

This book contains an extensive amount of quotes from Allen's writings. Rather than simply write about what Allen said, I have provided you with the primary sources. As much as possible, I have allowed him to speak for himself. At the conclusion of each chapter, you will find a list of endnotes to guide your future readings. Much of chapter one was taken from an article that I wrote several years ago for *The Churchman*.[2] And much of the rest of this book contains portions of my dissertation and an article that I published in the *Journal of the American Society for Church Growth*.[3] While I have published several books through traditional means, this one is the first of its kind that I have self-published. I decided to go this route because I wanted to release this book in 2012 in time for the anniversary of *Missionary Methods*; and I made this decision at the end of last year. Time was not on my side.

Interest in Roland Allen, especially in North America, has been growing in the last few years. I am very thankful for this reality. In my travels and conversations with others, I am finding more and more people agreeing that Allen has had a significant influence on their lives. I am finding that younger generations are reading Allen's works and recognizing that the Lord of the Harvest desires the gospel to spread rapidly and with honor (2 Thes 3:1).

I must state my appreciation to my wife Sarah and our children Hannah, Rachel, and Joel. They are a tremendous blessing and an encouragement to me in my writing endeavors. Their prayers are always coveted for such projects. I must also offer a word of appreciation to Amber Walsh who assisted in several administrative matters related to the publication of this book. Thank you Bette Smyth for your proofreading labors related to this book. Above all else, none of this work would have been possible without the grace of the Lord. May glory be given to Him.

J. D. Payne
March 2012

---

[1]Roland Allen, *Missionary Methods: St. Paul's or Ours?* American ed. (Grand

[2] J. D. Payne, "The Legacy of Roland Allen," *Chruchman* 117, no. 4 (Winter 2003): 315-28. Used with permission.

[3] J. D. Payne, "Missiology of Roland Allen," *Journal of the American Society for Church Growth* 15 (Winter 2004): 45-118. Used with permission.

Introduction to Spontaneous Expansion

Roland Allen was a prolific writer. During his lifetime, he authored numerous books, pamphlets, and articles. Upon examination of Allen's writings regarding the Church,[1] the reader encounters repeated themes. Allen was a master of redundancy. His repetition was necessary; in fact, it was strategic. We must remember that Allen was arguing against a long-standing missionary tradition.

The mission station approach to international missions was still in vogue.[2] The tenacity of the mission boards and missionaries was great, and one single writing against the problems of the day would not result in the needed paradigm shift. Though Allen continued to rehash many of the same arguments throughout his writings, he composed different variations on those repeated themes. It is not an understatement to say that Allen's missiology was—and in some contemporary situations still is—a radical missiology.

Allen himself was very much aware of his unusual views. His grandson, Hubert J. B. Allen, illustrated this awareness when he recalled, "When I was about twelve years old, asking my 'Grandfer' whether I could read his books, and receiving from him the reply: *Oh, yes, you can read them by all means—but you won't understand them; I don't think anyone is going to understand them until I've been dead ten years.*"[3] A misunderstood prophet is probably the best description of Allen during his lifetime.

Allen's convictions consisted of his desire to see the multiplication of disciples, leaders, and churches across the globe. The title of his other popular work, *The Spontaneous Expansion of the Church: And the Causes Which Hinder It*, revealed this passion. He did not believe that such growth was a complicated matter: "I delight to think that a Christian travelling on his business, or fleeing from persecution, could preach Christ, and a church spring up as the result of his preaching."[4] And while he was—and, in some cases—remains misunderstood, the simplicity behind the spontaneous expansion of the Church is evident:

> This then is what I mean by spontaneous expansion. I mean the expansion which follows the unexhorted and unorganized activity of individual members of the Church explaining to others the Gospel which they have found for themselves; I mean the expansion which follows the irresistible attraction of the Christian Church for men who see its ordered life, and are drawn to it by desire to discover the secret of a life which they instinctively desire to share; I mean also the expansion of the Church by the addition of new churches.[5]

But in order to understand properly such church growth, it is necessary to recognize where Allen's convictions rested.

Biblical and Theological Foundations

Prior to addressing Allen's missiology, the foundation on which his missiology was constructed must be understood. Harry R. Boer noted that "the methods which Allen advocated become quite meaningless apart from the theology out of which they arose."[6] In his article entitled "Roland Allen: Pioneer in a Spirit-Centered Theology of Mission," John E. Branner wrote: "It is my thesis that his methodology must not be divorced from his theology; to do so is an affront to the intentions of this man. His theology, particularly the emphasis on the work of the Holy Spirit, permeates his methodology and lays an indispensable foundation for it."[7]

There were four main components of Allen's missiological foundation. The first was Allen's understanding of the way of Christ. Though the majority of Allen's writings tend to focus on Acts and the Pauline corpus, Allen understood that the Lord's teachings were behind the expansion of the Apostolic Church. The second component was the apostolic approach. It was his examination of the New Testament that gained Allen much notoriety. He relied heavily on the New Testament for his theology. In fact, Branner observed that in all of Allen's major works there are only two brief Old Testament references.[8]

Derived from these two biblical aspects are the third and fourth theological components of Allen's missiology: eccelesiology and pneumatology. Allen came from an Anglican background and lived and died an Anglican. Though his ecclesiology obviously differed from others within his Church, the Anglican influence permeated his thoughts. The final component of his missiological foundation was his pneumatology. It was his Spirit-centered theology of mission that resulted in much controversy and branded him a radical during his day.

Though I have attempted to compartmentalize what I believe to be the four foundations on which Allen's theology resided, the reader must understand that these four components permeated all of Allen's thought. They wove themselves throughout his missiology like the threads of a tapestry. Boer was correct when he noted:

> When I speak of Allen's theology I do not refer to it in the sense in which we speak of Calvin's theology or Barth's theology. These latter are complete, systematic expositions of scripture and take fulsome note of the history of theology. Allen was not a theologian in this sense of the word. It is perhaps better not to refer to Allen as a theologian at all. I prefer to think of him as a keen student of the scriptures and as a missionary thinker.[9]

Allen did not leave behind a concise theology of mission; any theology discerned must be gleaned from his plethora of writings.[10]

[1] Unless otherwise noted, I will refer to the local church with a lowercase *c* and the universal, national, or denominational church with an uppercase *C*.

[2] A detailed description of the historical context of Allen's day and his mission situation is beyond the scope of this book. Others have addressed contextual issues in their biographical discussions. See Hubert J. B. Allen, *Roland Allen: Pioneer, Priest, and Prophet* (Cincinnati, OH: Forward Movement Publications; Grand Rapids, MI: William B. Eerdmans, 1995); William Nolan Burkhalter, "A Comparative Analysis of the Missiologies of Roland Allen and Donald Anderson McGavran" (Ph.D. diss., The Southern Baptist Theological Seminary, 1984), 63-85; Michael Don Thompson, "The Holy Spirit and Human Instrumentality in the Training of New Converts: An Evaluation of the Missiological Thought of Roland Allen" (Ph.D. diss., Golden Gate Baptist Theological Seminary, 1989), 8-77; John K. Branner, "Roland Allen, Donald McGavran and Church Growth" (Th.M. thesis, Fuller Theological Seminary, 1975), 1-7; and David M. Paton, ed., *Reform of the Ministry: A Study in the Work of Roland Allen* (London: Lutterworth Press, 1968), 13-45. Because the discussion of the controversies surrounding the mission station approach have been addressed and summarized in various writings over the twentieth century, I assume that the reader is familiar with the common-place methodology of Allen's day. I will discuss Allen's historical context only as it helps to shed light on certain aspects of his missiology. For information regarding a brief history and some problems with the mission station methodology, see Donald Anderson McGavran, *The Bridges of God: A Study in the Strategy of Missions* (New York, NY: Friendship Press, 1955), 42-67.

[3] Hubert J. B. Allen, Roland Allen, vii.

[4] Roland Allen, *The Spontaneous Expansion of the Church: And the Causes Which Hinder It*, American ed. (Grand Rapids, MI: Wm. B. Eerdmans, 1962), 7.

[5] Ibid.

[6] Harry R. Boer, "Roland Allen, the Holy Spirit, and Missions," *World Dominion* 33 (1955): 297.

---

[7] John E. Branner, "Roland Allen: Pioneer in a Spirit-Centered Theology of Mission," *Missiology* 5 (1977): 175-76.

[8] Ibid., 179.

[9] Boer, "Roland Allen, the Holy Spirit, and Missions," 299. It should be noted that despite the fact that Allen was not a systematician, he was well educated and theologically trained. He attended Bath College School and the Bristol Grammar School and won a scholarship to St. John's College, Oxford. In 1892 he was ordained a deacon and a year later became a priest. See Hubert J. B. Allen, *Roland Allen*, 17-20.

[10] Branner commented, "Whether one disagrees with Allen's theology or with his methodology does not alter the fact that he must be considered as a biblical theologian. . . . He was determined to be biblical in the spirit of Acts 17:11" (Branner, "Roland Allen: Pioneer in a Spirit-Centered Theology of Mission," 176).

Chapter 1
The Story of the Man[1]

One of the most controversial, yet most influential, missionary thinkers of all time was Roland Allen. An examination of his missionary work reveals nothing too impressive from a humanistic perspective. Rather, it was Allen's insights into the expansion of the Church that sometimes equated him as being a prophet, a revolutionary, a radical, or a troublemaker.

The Man[2]

Roland Allen was born to Charles Fletcher (1835-1873) and Priscilla (1839-1935) Allen in England on December 29, 1868. He was the sixth of seven children. At four weeks of age, he was baptized in St. Werburgh's Church. Charles graduated from Christ's College (Cambridge) in 1858 and served as a clergyman in the Church of England. While away from his family in 1873 in the colony of British Honduras, Charles died at the age of thirty-eight. Roland was not even five years of age.

As a young man, Roland won a scholarship to St. John's College (Oxford) and later won the university's Lothain prize for an essay on Pope Silvester II. While pursuing his studies, he was highly influenced by the Anglo-Catholic faculty at Pusey House near St. John's. Following college, Allen attended the high Anglican clergy training school in Leeds. He once commented: "When I was ordained, I was a child. My idea was to serve God in His Temple. Chiefly that, with a conviction that to be ignorant of God's Love revealed in Christ was to be in a most miserable state."[3] His principal described him as being "a refined intellectual man, small not vigorous, in no way burly or muscular . . . academic and fastidious. . . . [L]earning and civilization are more to him than most men."[4]

In 1892, Allen was ordained a deacon, and one year later became a priest and served his curacy in the Durham diocese in the parish of St. John the Evangelist, Darlington. Within a short period of time, Allen applied to the Society for the Propagation of the Gospel to serve as a missionary. Due to a certain heart condition, however, the Society refused to send him out as a missionary. Determined to begin missionary service as soon as possible, Allen, applied to the Society's associated mission, the independent Church of England to North China. Though his physical condition became an issue that appeared to thwart his opportunity to serve in China, Allen was able to convince his physician that he would not die in China any sooner than he would die in England. In 1894, Allen was accepted by the Mission and left for China after he completed his curacy in 1895.

After arriving in China, Allen opened a clergy school for a diocese in the Northern part of the country; he was involved in training boys to work as catechists. While serving in this school in Peking, Allen's views on education and leadership development were still status quo. While in China, he quickly learned Mandarin, and within a few years became a "3000-character man." He also oversaw both a day school for non-

Christians and a printing press and began a chaplaincy at the nearby Legation. Though he was involved in many roles, he nevertheless found time to write for the Mission's quarterly journal, *The Land of Sinim.*

The year 1900 was a dark time for Christians in China. Thousands of believers and many missionaries were killed due to the uprisings. Allen and his companions at the mission survived, but found themselves in the middle of the Boxer Rebellion and the ensuing siege that befell the Legation. Allen kept a dairy while in China, and his detailed record of the problems he experienced taking place at the turn of the twentieth century were published in 1901 under the title *The Siege of the Peking Legations.*[5]

Following the conflict in Peking, Allen returned to England for furlough. While at home, he served as a chaplain to the Bishop and represented his mission in China, which included raising funds for the mission stations that had been devastated. It was during this furlough in 1901 that Allen married Mary Beatrice Tarleton (1863-1960). They would eventually have two children: Priscilla Mary (1903-1987) and Iohn Willoughby Tarleton (1904-1979).

Allen and his wife departed to China in 1902. Allen's new service was to be at a mission station in Yung Ch'ing. It was during this time in China that Allen attempted to apply some of his missionary principles that contrasted with traditional missionary paternalism. He helped local believers to elect church councils and take more responsibility for finances, evangelism, and church leadership. Though his work was going well, his health deteriorated after nine months and he and his family were required to return to England. Though Allen wished to return to China, the Society did not grant that desire.

Having returned to England in 1903 and having recovered his health, Allen began serving as a vicar in the rural Buckinghamshire parish of Chalfont St. Peter in 1904. It was during this time that the writings of the apostle Paul made a dynamic impact on his thinking. He wrote: "I was ill, and came home for two years, and began to study the methods of the Apostle St. Paul. From that day forward I began to see light."[6]

Though Allen's wife thoroughly enjoyed her time at Chalfont St. Peter, in 1907 Allen resigned from his position for theological reasons.[7] This resignation revolved around the fact that Allen refused to carry out his duties of baptisms, marriages, and burial services to nonbelievers, practices that the Church of England required all priests to perform regardless of the nature of the person. Following this resignation, Allen did some deputation work for an overseas mission, occasionally assisted other clergy when they became ill, and spent much time thinking and writing.

In 1912, Allen published his classic work, *Missionary Methods: St. Paul's or Ours?* The title of the text revealed much about the book's content. Allen advocated that the missionary methods of the apostle were not antiquated, but rather should be applied to missionary endeavors in any day and time. Allen stated that "I myself am more convinced than ever that in the careful examination of his [St. Paul's] work, above all in the understanding and appreciation of his principles, we shall find the solution of most of our present difficulties."[8] Toward the end of the work, Allen poignantly wrote that "at any rate this much is certain, that the Apostle's methods succeeded exactly where ours have failed."[9]

The following year saw Allen's publication of *Missionary Principles*.[10] In this work Allen advocated that the indwelling Holy Spirit provides the missionary zeal. For Allen, the end of all missionary desire is a worldwide "Revelation of Christ."[11] It was his desire to discuss principles not only related to foreign missionary work but principles that "could be applied to any work anywhere."[12]

By 1914, many of Allen's missiological thoughts had been circulated via his writings. Two individuals that were sympathetic to his views were Sidney James Wells Clark, a wealthy Congregationalist layman, and Thomas Cochran, a Presbyterian Scotsman and missionary physician. Both men saw the value in Allen's thoughts as well as the importance of conducting surveys and other quantitative research to determine the needs of mission fields throughout the world.

Though the three men came from different denominational backgrounds, they all shared a desire to see contemporary missiological problems alleviated; and they all had a strong passion for the role of the Holy Spirit in the life of the Church and mission. Though Allen was not too fond of surveys and research, nevertheless, he joined forces with Clark and Cochran to become part of establishing the World Dominion

Movement in 1917. Hubert J. B. Allen noted the individual strengths of each man: "Their abilities complimented one another's: Clark's business acumen made him an excellent manager for the project; Cochrane's charm and sensitivity made him the team's diplomat; and Roland with his trained analytic mind and wide learning was their philosopher and theologian."[13] The following year, each man became involved in the Survey Application Trust and its publishing arm, the World Dominion Press.[14]

When World War I began in 1914, Allen served as a Naval chaplain onboard the Royal Fleet Auxiliary H.M.H.S. *Rohilla.* Allen's service was very brief due to an unfortunate violent shipwreck in which some of the crew died; Allen survived a death-defying swim to shore. After the war, Clark provided the Allen family with a house called Amenbury in Beaconsfield, west of London. He also provided the family with an honorarium of £200 so Allen could study international foreign missions. Allen believed that he published his best work in 1917, a small pamphlet entitled *Pentecost and the World.*[15] It was in this work that Allen attempted to address the missional nature of the Holy Spirit. He showed that the Holy Spirit, who came at Pentecost, was a Spirit who both empowered and motivated believers to propagate the gospel.

Allen's work *Educational Principles and Missionary Methods* was published in 1919. In his preface to the second edition of *Missionary Methods*, he stated that *Educational Principles and Missionary Methods* was written to address some of the criticisms against his thoughts in *Missionary Methods.* Allen also stressed that *Educational Principles and Missionary Methods* advocated that the greater the cultural/worldview distances between contemporary missionaries and the people to whom they minister, the greater the value of the apostolic method.[16]

During the 1920s, the Survey Application Trust issued a quarterly journal, *World Dominion.* Allen was a principal contributor to the periodical during this decade. In 1924, he conducted extensive survey work in Canada. Though Allen used the Trust's money to travel abroad to conduct research, his heart was never in survey work. Allen believed that the Trust should be about the promotion of indigenous church principles. His Canadian experience and several extended visits in the latter 1920's to Southern Africa and India shaped his missiology and confirmed for him many of his controversial thoughts.

It was during the 1920s that he wrote booklets and pamphlets such as *Voluntary Clergy* (1923), *Voluntary Clergy Overseas—an Answer to the Fifth World Call* (1928), and *Non Professional Missionaries* (1929). Another major moment in the 1920s occurred in 1927 when Allen published his book *The Spontaneous Expansion of the Church and the Causes Which Hinder It.* As the title suggested, this work included a discussion of the contemporary missiological barriers that prevented the natural expansion of the Church.

Allen was emotionally depressed in his latter years. If his depression was due to the fact that many did not widely accept his views, at least he acknowledged that he would probably never live to see his missiology implemented on a large scale. His grandson, Hubert J. B. Allen, remarked that his grandfather predicted that few would understand his views until ten years after his death.[17]

By 1930, Allen published *The Case for Voluntary Clergy.* David M. Paton suggested that this work was the incorporation in revised form of Allen's earlier works *Voluntary Clergy* and *Voluntary Clergy Overseas.*[18] Hubert J. B. Allen wrote that *The Case* "brought together and elaborated all Roland's principal arguments on this theme, at home and overseas."[19]

During the early 1930s, Allen and his wife desired to live closer to their children in Africa, so they moved from Amenbury to Nairobi. While in Africa, Allen conducted some survey work regarding the Anglican Church in Kenya and occasionally preached to different congregations. It was also during this decade that Allen decided to occasionally assist with the services at St. Mark's Church in Nairobi's Parklands suburb. Though Allen desired to see a regular clergyman appointed from within the people of St. Mark's Church, his desire soon turned to frustration. Hubert J. B. Allen noted that "after a while he began to express exasperation that the church members kept expecting him to 'fill gaps', instead of persuading the Bishop to appoint the 'voluntary clergy' that he advocated."[20] Since Allen believed he was hindering the congregation by keeping them content in the status quo, he withdrew himself from St. Mark's Church, exactly thirty-two years after his resignation from Chalfont St. Peter.[21] While in Kenya, Allen continued to write. In 1937, he published a biography about Sidney James Wells Clark entitled *S.J.W. Clark: A Vision of Missions.* He also decided to learn Swahili and translated and published several Swahili writings into English.

At seventy-nine years of age, Allen was very ill. Despite his health, Priscilla Allen commented: "His mind remained clear and alert until the morning before his death, and he died without pain."[22] Allen died on June 9, 1947. His funeral was conduced by the Bishop of Mombasa. Allen's gravestone can be found in Nairobi's City Park. A simple stone cross with the inscription on the pedestal reads:

ROLAND ALLEN
Clerk in Holy Orders
1868-1947
I AM the Resurrection and the Life Saith the Lord[23]

---

[1] This chapter originally appeared in *Churchman*, vol. 117, no. 4, (Winter 2003): 315-328, as part of the article *The Legacy of Roland Allen.* It is used here by permission.

[2] The only extensive biography of Roland Allen was published by his grandson: Hubert J. B. Allen, *Roland Allen: Pioneer, Priest, and Prophet* (Cincinnati, OH: Forward Movement Publications; Grand Rapids, MI: Wm. B. Eerdmans Publishing Co., 1995). Unless otherwise noted, all biographical information found in this chapter was taken from Hubert J. B. Allen's superior work. Other excellent, yet less extensive, biographical writings regarding Roland Allen can be found in *Reform of the Ministry: A Study in the Work of Roland Allen*, ed. David M. Paton (London: Lutterworth Press, 1968), 11-45; Noel Q. King, "Last Years in East Africa," in *Reform of the Ministry: A Study in the Work of Roland Allen*, ed. David M. Paton (London: Lutterworth Press, 1968), 165-77; Alexander McLeish, "Biographical Memoir," in *The Ministry of the Spirit: Selected*

Writings of Roland Allen, ed. David M. Paton (Grand Rapids, MI: William B. Eerdmans, 1960), ix-xvi.

[3] J. B. Hubert Allen, *Roland Allen: Pioneer, Priest, and Prophet* (Cincinnati, OH: Forward Movement Publications; Grand Rapids, MI: Wm. B. Eerdmans, 1995), 19.

[4]Ibid.

[5] Roland Allen, *The Siege of the Peking Legations* (London: Smith Elder and Company, 1901). The proceeds from *Seige*, Allen's first publication, went to help raise money for the Mission, following all the destruction experienced by the Chinese.

[6] J. B. Hubert Allen citing Roland Allen in *Church Missionary Review* (June 1927): : 75. Unfortunately, Hubert Allen did not provide the full bibliographic information of the *Church Missionary Review* article.

[7] Allen's resignation letter can be found in Hubert J. B. Allen's book, pages 183-88.

[8] Roland Allen, *Missionary Methods: St. Paul's or Ours?* Reprinted American ed., (Grand Rapids, MI: William B. Eerdmans, 1998), vii.

[9] Ibid., 147.

[10] Published in New York under the title *Essential Missionary Principles.*

[11] Roland Allen, *Missionary Principles* (Grand Rapids, MI: William B. Eerdmans, 1964), 137.

[12] Ibid., 167.

[13]Ibid., 93.

[14] The Survey Application Trust and the World Dominion Press were established to spread the missiological thoughts of Clark and Allen throughout the world.

[15] David M. Paton republished most of this work in his book *The Ministry of the Spirit* (Grand Rapids, MI: William B. Eerdmans, 1960), 1-61.

[16] Allen, *Missionary Methods*, vii, viii.

[17] Ibid., 165.

[18] Paton, *The Ministry of the Spirit*, 136. Paton's work contains several chapters of *The Case for Voluntary Clergy*.

[19] Ibid., 146.

[20] Ibid., 157.

[21] Hubert Allen's work includes a copy of Allen's letter withdrawing from St. Mark's Church on November 26, 1939. See page 215-216.

[22] Priscilla M. Allen, "Roland Allen: A Prophet for this Age," *The Living Church* 192, no.16 (April 20, 1986): 11.

[23] Hubert Allen has included a small black and white photograph of this gravestone in his work. See page 230.

Chapter 2
Way of Jesus

In a brief article entitled "New Testament Missionary Methods," Allen examined some of the New Testament teachings in relation to the work of the missionary and the church. According to Allen, the first sending of missionaries as done by Christ revealed some important facts to consider.[1] For Allen, these facts differed from the contemporary practices of his day.

First, Allen observed that Christ taught the apostles by both word and deed. According to Allen, Christ's training was not theoretical or in the confines of an institution separated from the missionary task. "He trained them in the work, not outside it; in the world, not in a hothouse."[2] A second fact regarding Christ's approach to the missionary is bound up in the charge "Go not into the way of the Gentiles and into any city of the Samaritans enter ye not: but go rather to the lost sheep of the house of Israel"; and the missionary is (1) to go preaching, (2) to go healing, raising the dead, casting out demons, (3) to go without provision, (4) to accept hospitality, (5) to turn away openly from those who refuse to hear.[3] Commenting on this charge, Allen stated:

> We must observe that the direction not to go to Gentiles or Samaritans was obviously only for that time; the direction to heal was not to use the art of a physician but the faith of an exorcist; the direction to go without

> provision was only for that time, because it was later definitely withdrawn (Luke 22:35); the direction to accept hospitality is connected closely with the acceptance of their peace, as the direction to turn away from those who refused hospitality is connected with the refusal to hear them. Where the message of Christ is refused a moral hearing, there it is a moral duty to refuse to continue to repeat it. We see this in the practice of St. Paul (Acts 18:6).[4]

Though Allen never referred to the principle of receptivity in name, it is evident that he was aware of the principle behind this fact.

A final fact about Christ and the missionary is related to the statement, "The laborer is worthy of his hire," which was given before the sending out of the seventy. Allen interpreted this biblical practice to be quite different from the contemporary practice of missionary financial compensation. According to Allen: "That applies to wandering messengers, bidding them accept hospitality, and is quite different from a direction that missionaries should be paid a salary—a thing abhorrent in the eyes of early Christians (cf. The denunciation of a salary by Apollonius quoted in Eusebius H. E. V. 18.2)."[5]

Allen viewed Christ as being greatly concerned that believers were to be incorporated into an earthly society, the church. According to Allen: "That Christ did not contemplate only the conversion of a number of men and women who believed in Him, but also their establishment as a society upon earth, is seen both in his references to the Church in His speech, and even more clearly in His ordinance of baptism, a rite of admission to a society, and of the Lord's Supper, a rite of communion in the society."[6]

Summary

For Allen, the way of Christ was the archetype of mission for the Apostolic Church. Regarding His approach, Allen stressed:

> The Apostles followed Christ in this; they established a society, a spiritual society on earth. The establishment of this society is most clearly seen in the work and writing of the Apostle Paul. He recognized a Church; he established churches.[7]

It is easy to understand how someone could look at Allen's work and focus on the Pauline elements influencing his missiology. Allen, time and again, supported his arguments with evidence from the apostle Paul; he rarely discussed the way of Christ. Despite the small quantity of Allen's material centered on the christological approach, the researcher must not forget that Allen knew the background of the Apostolic Church.[8] In his work *Pentecost and the World*, he wrote:

> The same Holy Spirit which descended upon Christ was to descend upon them [apostles]. The same Spirit which in Jesus fulfilled the commandment of the Father to come into the world was in the apostles to fulfil the commandment to "Go into all the world." Thus the work of the apostles with which this book is concerned is linked with the work of Jesus Christ as the carrying on of that which He began on earth under the impulse of the same Spirit through whom He acted and spoke.[9]

The apostles observed, interacted with, and were equipped by Jesus Himself. What the apostle Paul was not able to experience first hand, because he was "one untimely born" (1 Cor 15:8), he was able to gain though his encounters with the Twelve and others who had been influenced by the Jerusalem church in some fashion.

---

1 Roland Allen, "New Testament Missionary Methods," *The Missionary Review of the World* 52 (1929): 21.

2 Ibid.

3 Ibid.

4 Ibid.

5 Ibid., 21-22.

6 Ibid., 22.

7 Ibid.

[8] Hubert J. B. Allen noted that Allen—whatever the point of discussion, would –often respond to his critics with the phrase "This is the way of Christ and His Apostles." See Hubert J. B. Allen, *Roland Allen*, 172.

[9] Roland Allen, *Pentecost and the World: The Revelation of the Holy Spirit in the "Acts of the Apostles,"* in *The Ministry of the Spirit: Selected Writings of Roland Allen*, American ed., ed. David M. Paton, (Grand Rapids, MI: William B. Eerdmans, 1962), 6.

Chapter 3
The Apostolic Approach

Allen frequently referred to the apostolic approach to missionary practice. His hero was no doubt the apostle Paul. The title of Allen's most famous work, *Missionary Methods: St. Paul's or Ours?*, revealed the level of esteem to which he held the apostle's practice. The following are various quotations showing the importance of the apostolic approach to Allen's overall missiology.

In a work entitled *Mission Activities Considered in Relation to the Manifestation of the Spirit*, Allen reminded his readers of the vast difference between modern mission practices and the apostolic approach.

> That missionaries should set out to inaugurate and conduct social reforms is so familiar to us that we scarcely question it; but if we look at the New Testament account of the work of the Apostles, we see at once how strange it appears. If we try to imagine St. Paul, for instance, setting out to serve the people of Macedonia in the sense in which we set out to serve the peoples of China or of Africa . . . we find that we cannot imagine any such thing. And the reason? . . . [I]t is because there is a great gulf between our idea of direct social service as the work of a missionary of the Gospel and his conception of his work as a missionary of the Gospel.[1]

Allen also challenged his readers to critique contemporary methodologies by the apostolic approach. In writing *Discussion on Mission Education*, Allen argued:

> We are carrying on this educational work because it is one of the policies of our board. But boards are not infallible. It is one of the most difficult things in the world to change the outlook of a group of people who have got into a rut, or whose policy is heavily involved in property considerations. But let us face this thing openly and honestly. Are we following the Apostolic way, the most successful way, of extending the Church, or are we employing a method which experience has proved to many people to be a conspicuous failure?[2]

Allen was not ashamed to confess that he believed the apostolic way held the key to unlocking many modern missiological problems. In the preface to the second (1927) edition of *Missionary Methods: St. Paul's or Ours?*, he reflected:

> It is now fifteen years since this book was first published, and it is thought that a new and cheaper edition may be useful. In these fifteen years I have seen, and I have heard from others, that action in many parts of the world has been influenced by the study of St. Paul's missionary methods; and I myself am more convinced than ever that in the careful examination of his work, above all in the

understanding and appreciation of his principles, we shall find the solution of most of our present difficulties.[3]

Within the same text, Allen made a poignant statement revealing his bias toward the apostolic approach. Regarding the establishment of churches, he advocated that

> we must allow to his methods a certain character of universality, and now I venture to urge that, since the Apostle, no other has discovered or practised methods for the propagation of the Gospel better than his or more suitable to the circumstances of our day. It would be difficult to find any better model than the Apostle in the work of establishing new churches. At any rate this much is certain, that the Apostle's methods succeeded exactly where ours have failed.[4]

This apostolic approach of establishing a church could be summarized in the following lengthy quotation:

> Four things, then we see St. Paul deemed necessary for the establishment of his churches, and only four. A tradition or elementary Creed, the Sacraments of Baptism and the Holy Communion, Orders, and the Holy Scriptures. He trained his converts in the simplest and most practical form. He delivered these to them. He exercised them as a body in the understanding and practice of them, and he

left them to work them out for themselves as a body whilst he himself went on with his own special work. He was ready at any moment to encourage or direct them by messengers, by letters, or by personal visits, as they needed direction or encouragement; but he neither desired, nor attempted, to stay with them, or to establish his ministers amongst them to do for them what he was determined that they must learn to do for themselves. He knew the essential elements, and he trained his converts in those and in those alone, and he trained them by teaching them to use what he gave them.[5]

For Paul, leaving behind these four necessities required him to follow two principles. First, he was a preacher of the gospel and not of any system of law. Paul came to "administer a spirit. . . . He did not establish a constitution, he inculcated principles. He did not introduce any practice to be received on his own or any human authority, he strove to make his converts realize and understand its relation to Christ."[6] Paul realized that the power of Christ that was within himself was the same power that was within the lives of the infant churches. The apostle was convinced that they had been blessed with "every spiritual blessing" and were complete in Christ.[7] The same Spirit who guided Paul was the same Sprit who was able to guide the infant congregations to follow the same example that Paul had modeled.[8]

The second principle was that Paul practiced "retirement."[9] Paul established the church and intentionally moved on to repeat the process. The apostle understood any new church to be just as legitimate as any well-established local church. Paul's retirement was done to help the church exercise "the powers which they possessed in Christ. He warned them of dangers, but he did not provide an elaborate machinery to prevent them from succumbing to the dangers."[10] Paul had confidence in the Holy Spirit who had baptized the infant believers.

Summary

Michael Don Thompson was correct when he wrote that "Allen found in Paul the perfect prototype of the missionary who believed wholeheartedly in the power of Christ, and then lived and ministered in a way which clearly reflected that belief."[11] John Branner observed that in the years following the publication of *Missionary Methods: St. Paul's or Ours?* (1912), Allen's primary emphasis in his writings became "How did Paul do it?"[12] It was Allen's quest to find the answer to this question that resulted in much opposition and misunderstanding from his readers.

Branner commented that Allen was not one who developed nice theories, but rather was concerned with the practice of Pauline principles. Allen's development of Pauline methods was derived from the Pauline principles.[13] In fact, Branner stated that Allen was probably a "Pauline pragmatist" who felt that Paul's "principles were the ideal and because of that they were practical."[14] To establish indigenous churches, we must follow Pauline principles.[15] More will be discussed regarding the apostolic approach in chapter six.

---

[1] Roland Allen, *Mission Activities Considered in Relation to the Manifestation of the Spirit* (London: World Dominion Press, 1927), 21-22.

[2] Roland Allen, *Discussion on Mission Education* (London: World Dominion Press, 1931), 14.

[3] Roland Allen, *Missionary Methods: St. Paul's or Ours?*, American ed. (Grand Rapids, MI: Wm. B. Eerdmans, 1962), vii.

[4] Ibid., 147.

[5] Ibid., 107.

[6] Ibid., 148, 149.

[7] Ephesians 1:3.

[8] Allen, *Missionary Methods,* 149.

[9] Ibid.

[10] Ibid.

[11] Michael Don Thompson, "The Holy Spirit and Human Instrumentality in the Training of New Converts: An Evaluation of the Missiological Thought of Roland Allen" (Ph.D. diss., Golden Gate Baptist Theological Seminary, 1989), 69-70.

[12] John K. Branner, "Roland Allen, Donald McGavran and Church Growth," (Th.M. thesis, Fuller Theological Seminary, 1975), 22.

[13] Ibid., 26.

[14] Ibid.

[15] Ibid.

Chapter 4
Ecclesiology

John Branner was correct when he observed, "One might think that the ecclesiology of such a man would be easy to identify. But this is certainly not the case."[1] In the process of deciphering Allen's ecclesiology, two reoccurring streams of thought that relate to his missiology continue to flow. First, he held the Eucharist and the other rites in high esteem, and second, he emphasized the indigenous concept. Both of these strains of thought were bound up into Allen's understanding of Church. For a congregation to be a church, it had to be able to participate in the divine rites of the Church while simultaneously exist in an indigenous state of being.

Eucharist

It was his Anglican upbringing that shaped his understanding of the Eucharist. Concerning Allen's early days, David M. Paton wrote:

> Allen started life, as we have seen, as a High Churchman in the Tractarian tradition. It was the now old-fashioned Anglican Catholicism—sober, restrained, scholarly, immensely disciplined. There is no trace anywhere in him of the preoccupation with secondary matters of ceremony into which the high Tractarian position sometimes

> degenerated. He went to the North China Mission of the SPG at Peking. There is no trace in the records of any disagreement, while he was a member of the Mission, with its sober and courteous but firmly felt and taught High Churchmanship.[2]

Paton continued, "He never loses his profound belief that the Eucharist is utterly necessary to any group of Christians, large or small, as the essential centre of their common life."[3] Allen himself proclaimed:

> A body which cannot perform its own proper rites is not a Church. To call it by that name is unreal: it is spiritually false. To pretend that men for whom a "Chaplain" turns up at intervals to hold a service enjoy Church life is self-deception.[4]

The controversy regarding the necessity of voluntary clergy,(which will be addressed in chapter ten) was founded on this belief in the necessity of the Eucharist. In the Anglican tradition, a minister was needed for the proper administration of the Eucharist. If the Anglican Church did not have enough money to provide a minister for a group of believers located in some remote part of a country or if no minister could be found, those believers could not participate in the Eucharist. For Allen, to prevent a body of believers from participating in this rite was tantamount to heresy. For, in the words of Paton, "It is in the doing of the Eucharist that they are the Church."[5]

Drawing from the night before the Passion event, Allen reminded his readers of the ordinance of Christ:

> When we are told that Christ ordained his Last Supper as a rite to be observed by all his people, when we are told that two Sacraments are generally necessary to Salvation, but are also told by the same teachers that Christians must not observe the Lord's Supper, that they must not offer their Eucharist, unless they can secure the services of one of that small body of professional clerics. . . . The observance of the Lord's Supper appears not the proper rite of Christian men, but a spiritual luxury appreciated by individuals.[6]

For Allen, all churches, from their inception, must be able to observe the ordinances.[7] A priest was not necessary because Christ is the Priest. "Is it true?" Allen asked, "that in the Eucharist Christ is the Priest, and that God alone can consecrate the elements of bread and wine, that the faithful who partake of them may be united to Christ, feeding upon him?"[8] Elsewhere Allen stressed:

> The Christian Eucharist is a great bond of fellowship. No Christian ought to be deprived of that fellowship. The Christian Eucharist is a great song of Redemption. No

> Christian should be forbidden to sing it. The Christian Eucharist is a great witness to the world, a proclamation of the Gospel. No Christian ought to be hindered from bearing that witness and proclaiming that Gospel by his observance of it. And I say that this is in accordance with the mind of Christ, and the will of God revealed to us in Christ.[9]

Indigenous

The second important element to Allen's ecclesiology was his understanding of the indigenous nature of the local church. As Paton observed: "The heart of Allen's understanding is that the Church lives by faith in Christ, whose gifts are sufficient for its life. At every level the Church is empowered by Christ to be itself, from the almost illiterate little congregation in a village to the Vatican Council itself; and the deepest considerations apply as much to the one as to the other, and to all other levels between."[10]

Once again, Allen's thoughts in this area were derived from the apostolic approach.

> Now if we look at the work of St. Paul, I think it must be perfectly clear that the local Churches of his foundation were essentially what we call native Churches. The little groups of Christians that he established in towns like Lystra or Derbe, Thessalonica or Beroea, were wholly

> composed of permanent residents in the country. They managed their own internal affairs under the leadership of their own officers, they administered their own sacraments, they controlled their own finance, and they propagated themselves, establishing in neighbouring towns or villages Churches like themselves. They were, in fact, Churches; and if Churches of that character which I have described are not what we mean by native Churches, then I do not know what meaning that term can possibly have. As these Churches multiplied provincial organization grew up, and that was native because the elements out of which it grew were native.[11]

Nothing foreign and, in Allen's case, nothing Western, must be projected onto the native church for it to be indigenous.

In 1927, he penned an article for *The International Review of Missions* entitled "The Use of the Term 'Indigenous.'" It was in this writing that he addressed the proper and improper understandings of using the term to refer to the local church.

In the strict sense of the word, Allen did not believe that a church could be indigenous. As Allen showed at the beginning of the article, whenever someone turns to an English dictionary for the definition of the word *indigenous*, the definition is similar to something born in a country, arising out of the soil of a particular area, or natural to the region. It was this concept of being natural to a region that Allen refused to believe could be applied to a church.

> In the natural sense of the strict definition, aboriginal, neither Christianity nor the Church can be said to be indigenous in any particular country in the world; for we know the date of its introduction into every country. In the land where it first appeared it did not spring out of the soil naturally, but was introduced supernaturally at a late date, and it established itself most firmly not in the country where it first appeared but in countries into which it was imported later."[12]

In the proper sense, a church can never be indigenous; the church was never natural to an area. The church was and is foreign. The church was an intruder.

Despite this semantic impossibility, Allen understood that a church could be indigenous if viewed from both a spiritual perspective and from a growth perspective. Just as Christ incarnated Himself and established the Church in Palestine, which began to grow across the world, the gospel and the Church are spiritually indigenous everywhere.[13] It is this supernatural establishment and expansion that Allen viewed as the proper manner to speak of the indigenous church.

Like many of his predecessors, Allen saw the indigenous church as consisting of the familiar terms: *self-governing*, *self-supporting*, and *self-extending*. Concerning the word *indigenous*, Allen noted: "It certainly does seem to embrace these three terms, because it seems impossible to think of any living thing as indigenous in a country, unless it can support its own life in the country, and that is self-support; unless it can direct its own conduct so as to maintain itself, and that is self-government; and unless it can propagate itself on the soil which is self-extension."[14]

Allen emphasized that the growth must not be controlled from an outside source. He stated that "we cannot possibly call anything indigenous which does not grow and spread of its own inherent vitality."[15] He further commented:

> It is essentially in its spontaneous growth and propagation that Christianity, or the Church, is revealed in its true character as indigenous in every country. If we want to know whether anything is indigenous anywhere, we must see it free; if we want to know what its character as indigenous is, we must see how it behaves when in a free condition. Only its spontaneous activity shows us whether it is indigenous, or what it is.[16]

It was in the understanding of spontaneous expansion that Allen primarily saw the local church being indigenous. He wrote that "this is what I understand by an indigenous Church: I understand a Church which possesses as inherent in itself everything which is essential to the existence of a Church, and is able to multiply itself without any necessary reference to any external authority."[17]

This unaided replication process was grounded in Allen's understanding of the simple nature of the Church:

> In the New Testament the idea of a Church is simple. It is an organized body of Christians in a place with its [leaders]. The Christians with their officers are the Church in the place, and they are addressed as such. This is simple and intelligible. That Church is the visible Body of Christ in the place, and it has all the rights and privileges and duties of the Body of Christ. Above it is the Universal Church, composed of all the Churches in the world, and of all the redeemed in heaven and on earth. The Apostolic idea of the Church is wonderfully intelligible to men everywhere. . . . The Apostolic system is so simple, that it can be apprehended by men in every stage of education, and civilization.[18]

Allen exposed the myth that an indigenous church is one that manifests a particular cultural practice that is found among the people of the particular church.

> To jump to the conclusion that a Church is indigenous because it practises some local custom or expresses its faith in some purely local form, is simply an example of the proneness of men to judge by externals, and often by trivial externals. No Church can be indigenous which is not propagating itself on the soil. To ignore that, and to imagine that local variation is a proof of indigenous character, is fatal. The variation must come out of the persistent and vigorous propagation of itself on the soil;

> then, and then only, is it a symptom of indigenous character.[19]

Just because a church worshipped in a certain style, sang to a certain genre of music, dressed in a particular manner, or had a certain order of service did not make that church indigenous.

The term *indigenous* as applied to a church referred to three concepts. First, the Church is "spiritually and eternally proper to all countries and peoples in the world." Second, the Church's "spiritual fitness for this or that particular country or people appears in time." Third, the Church "makes itself at home, that it grows and expands on the soil without any external aid, spontaneously."[20]

---

[1] John E. Branner, "Roland Allen: Pioneer in a Spirit-Centered Theology of Mission," *Missiology* 5 (1977): 178.

[2] David M. Paton, "Roland Allen: A Biographical and Theological Essay," in *Reform of the Ministry: A Study in the Word of Roland Allen,* ed. David M. Paton (London: Lutterworth Press, 1968), 24.

[3] Ibid., 25.

[4] Roland Allen, "The Priesthood of the Church," *The Church Quarterly Review* 115 (1933): 237.

[5] Paton, "Roland Allen: A Biographical and Theological Essay," 25.

[6] Allen, "The Priesthood of the Church," 237-38.

[7] Branner, commenting on Allen's ecclesiology, stated: "Hence, as the local church was planted on the mission field and partook of the sacraments it was

giving evidence of its inclusion in the Church." See Branner, "Roland Allen: Pioneer in a Spirit-Centered Theology of Mission," 178.

[8] Allen, "The Priesthood of the Church," 240.

[9] Ibid., 241. It should be noted that Allen did not discard local church leadership. In fact, Allen once stated: "St. Paul, as I understand his action, was convinced that a native Church requires duly appointed ministers, and in this sense there was no local Church until they were appointed." See Roland Allen, "Essentials of an Indigenous Church," *World Dominion* 3 (1925): 114.

[10] Paton, "Roland Allen: A Biographical and Theological Essay," 26.

[11] Roland Allen, "The Essentials of an Indigenous Church," *World Dominion* 3 (1925): 111.

[12] Ibid., 240.

[13] Roland Allen, "The Use of the Term 'Indigenous,'" *The International Review of Missions* 16 (1927): 262.

[14] Ibid.

[15] Ibid., 263.

[16] Ibid., 263-64.

[17] Roland Allen, "The Essentials of an Indigenous Church," *The Chinese Recorder* 56 (1925): 496.

[18] Roland Allen, "Devolution: The Question of the Hour," *World Dominion* 5 (1927): 283-84.

[19] Allen, "The Use of the Term 'Indigenous,'" 266.

[20] Ibid., 264.

Chapter 5
Pneumatology

Though Allen's development of the indigenous concept continued from where Henry Venn, Rufus Anderson, and John Nevius left off, it was Allen who rediscovered the approach to looking at missions in light of the Spirit.[1] Charles Chaney suggested that Allen's understanding of the Spirit "was probably Allen's most important contribution to missiological theory and the most distinctive thrust of his thought."[2] John Branner observed that "the gift of the Holy Spirit to believers was something which was to govern Allen's entire concept of mission, particularly that of the indigenous church."[3]

For Allen, the Spirit was the one who led the Church to do mission. So vital was the role of the Spirit in Allen's thinking that he wrote a small booklet entitled *Pentecost and the World: The Revelation of the Holy Spirit in the "Acts of the Apostles"* (1917). It was in this work that Allen delineated his understanding of the role of the Spirit in missionary practice. In the first chapter of the work, Allen expressed his understanding of the Holy Spirit in the book of Acts:

> The Holy Spirit is first given, then all the acts are described as consequences of His descent upon human beings. If we read the book in this way, then we see not the consequences of familiar human instincts and qualities, but the consequences which follow the giving of the Holy

> Spirit to men already possessed of these instincts and qualities. We see what happens when the Holy Spirit descends upon men of like passions with ourselves. Loyalty to Christ did not drive the apostles to abandon the religious privileges of their race and the traditions of their fathers in order to embrace heathen Gentiles within the fold of the Church. Zeal for Christ's honour did not teach them how to approach those heathen and to establish the Church. It was the Holy Spirit, the Spirit of the Redeemer, which did this. From this point of view their words and acts become a wonderful revelation of the Holy Spirit.[4]

It is our grasping of the vital truth about this missionary Spirit that is necessary for a proper understanding of life in the Church. Referring to Acts 1:8, Allen mentioned that Luke focused the reader's attention on the internal Spirit, rather than an external command to bear witness to the Christ. Allen made note of the fact that Luke speaks "not of men who, being what they were, strove to obey the last orders of a beloved Master, but of men who, receiving a Spirit, were driven by that Spirit to act in accordance with the nature of that Spirit."[5]

Though Christ gave the Great Commission, Allen believed that had the words never been spoken, the Church would have continued to go and preach. He argued this point:

> It would be far more true to say that had the Lord not given any such command, had the Scriptures never contained such a form of words, or could Christians blot it out from their Bibles and from their memories, the obligation to preach the Gospel to all nations would not have been diminished by a single iota. For the obligation depends not upon the letter, but upon the Spirit of Christ; not upon what He orders, but upon what He is, and the Spirit of Christ is the Spirit of Divine love and compassion and desire for souls astray from God.[6]

The Spirit who was given to the apostles "created in them an internal necessity to preach the Gospel. 'We cannot but speak,' they say."[7]

The Spirit was not given for the believer to enjoy alone. The reception of the Spirit was the reception of one who would motivate and move the Church to action.

> When once a man has admitted the all-embracing Sprit of Redeeming Love he can no longer look upon the Church as an institution designed to supply certain spiritual and social needs of the people here. . . . The moment that we recognize the Spirit in us as a Spirit of missions, we know that we are not partakers of Christ for ourselves alone, we know that the Church which does not conquer the world dies. . . . But the apprehension of the Spirit of Christ as a

missionary Spirit . . . also drives us to look beyond the bounds of our own Communion.[8]

---

[1] I say "rediscovered" because there is nothing new under the sun. According to Allen, all that he advocated regarding the Holy Spirit in missions had been taught and practiced by the Apostolic and Early Church.

[2] Charles Chaney, "Roland Allen: The Basis of His Missionary Principles and His Influence Today," *Occasional Bulletin* 14, no. 5 (May 1963): 5.

[3] John E. Branner, "Roland Allen: Pioneer in a Spirit-Centered Theology of Mission," *Missiology* 5 (1977): 181.

[4] Roland Allen, *Pentecost and the World: The Revelation of the Holy Spirit in the "Acts of the Apostles,"* in *The Ministry of the Spirit: Selected Writings of Roland Allen*, American ed., ed. David M. Paton (Grand Rapids, MI: William B. Eerdmans, 1962), 4.

[5] Ibid., 5.

[6] Roland Allen, *Essential Missionary Principles* (New York: Flemming H. Revell Company, 1913), 67.

[7] Roland Allen, *Pentecost and the World*, 27.

[8] Roland Allen, *Missionary Principles* (Grand Rapids, MI: William B. Eerdmans, 1964), 144-45.

Chapter 6
Place of the Missionary

The focus of the missionary was to be on three priorities:

- evangelism
- apostolic approach
- the Ministration of the Spirit.

In Allen's mind, these three priorities were bound together by what he referred to as missionary "faith" and all three were to remain in focus in every context missionaries found themselves (see Figure 1).

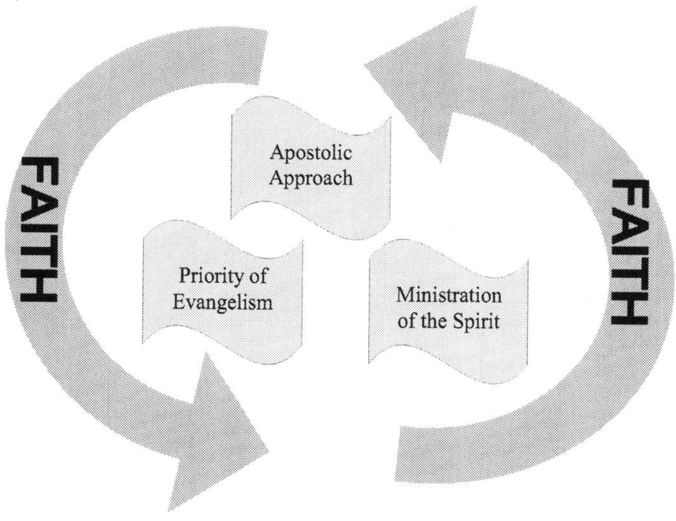

Figure 1. The Role of the Missionary

Priority of Evangelism

Allen spent some of his time addressing the relationship between evangelistic, medical, and educational mission work. He lived during a time when the controversy between evangelism and social involvement was on the rise. A "demise of evangelicalism" was the result of the World Missionary Conference at Edinburgh (1910) and at the Jerusalem Conference eighteen years later.

> The Gospel was seen as a way of life, not only a subject for belief. Deeds, they said, must precede proclamation. This new emphasis, however, was not only pragmatic but also a result of the triumph of "modernism" and liberal theology. It was the consequence resulting from a lower view of the Bible. . . . [T]he witness of social action was necessary in order to give evangelistic credibility.[1]

Despite the cultural decline in the primacy of evangelism in mission work, Allen did not shift with the times. In an article he penned in 1920 entitled "The Relation between Medical, Educational and Evangelistic Work in Foreign Missions," he wrote:

> Of the reasons for supporting evangelistic missions I need not speak at length. I believe that they are in themselves supreme, and that without them no educational or medical missions would ever have come into existence. . . . Christ, the beginning, the end; the need for Christ; the hope in

> Christ; the desire for His glory; the conviction of His sovereignty; the impulse of His Spirit—these are some of the reasons for evangelistic missions, and, however we may express them, they are, as I said, in their nature supreme.[2]

Though he was supportive of medical and educational mission work, he believed that they were not to be divorced from or dominate evangelism. Allen continued his emphasis on evangelism to the point of stating that the need which evangelistic missions meet in people's lives is "the supreme need" and by asking the rhetorical question, "May I, then, take it as agreed that evangelization is the supreme end of missions?"[3]

Not Results Oriented

Despite this priority of evangelism in mission activity, Allen did not support a focus that was results oriented. It was his conviction that when missionaries sought to manifest the revelation of Christ in a given culture, they would keep their practice in a proper perspective. For Allen, the only hope for proper missionary practice was Christ:

> The Spirit which impels to missionary labour is the Spirit of Christ. All missionary desire and effort proceed from the presence of Christ in the souls of His people. He is the only source; He also is the end. From Him proceeds the impulse; in Him it finds its fulfilment [*sic*]; to Him it

> moves. The Hope set before us in the manifestation of Christ, the unfolding of His nature, the demonstration of His power, the revelation of His glory. Our Hope is Jesus Christ.[4]

This revelation of Christ to others enabled missionaries to understand that they were not to be working toward an external result. As will be noted below, when the focus was on converts, church growth, or social reform, missionary practice became off-balance. The primary task of the missionary was the "unfolding of a Person."[5] Allen described this unfolding as a "revelation" in which missionaries have the confidence of success.

> We seek a revelation. A revelation is the unfolding of something that is, not the creation of something that is not. We are to have a part in the manifestation of the nature, the power, the grace of Christ, in the bringing back to the Father in Him of a world which has gone astray. But this is the unfolding of a mystery hid in God from all eternity, and complete from all eternity in Christ. In Christ the victory is already won; in Him the Saints are perfected; in Him the Church is complete. St. Paul told the Ephesian Christians that they were chosen in Christ before the foundation of the world. . . . Thus we do not seek to make that to be which is not, we seek to bring to light that which is. It is in Christ. It is the Father's will to reveal it. What calmness, what security, what hope, is here![6]

When this revelation of Christ failed to remain at the forefront of missionary thinking and practice, it was easy for the focus to become anthropocentric. If missionaries focused on converts, soon "men's souls begin to occupy our whole horizon. . . . [For] 'Converts' and 'Christ' are not identical."[7] Allen firmly believed that if missionaries thought in terms of converts, they would begin to exaggerate the importance of numbers.[8]

> But if we habitually rest in the "Christ" term numbers assume their proper place. The question which occupies the centre is not, How many? How few?; but Is Christ here being revealed? Can I find signs of Him? Numbers as "souls" do not cease to be important. There is no danger of careless indifference. We are more eager, not less. Yet the vice has gone out of numbers. The difference is startling.[9]

Allen was also concerned with missionaries who placed church growth as their utmost priority. The missionary, however, should understand that "it is only as a Revelation of Christ that the perfecting of the Church has any meaning."[10] Just as missionaries could not make the conversion of individuals their sole aim, church extension could not be the highest priority. The danger of focusing on the growth of the church was that "it is possible to make the institution the end."[11] For Allen, the focus had to remain on Christ and not the extension of the Church.

But is not the extension of the church synonymous with the revelation of Christ? According to Allen, the answer was no. He addressed this issue:

> It is easy to say they are the same, because the manifestation of Christ is in and through the perfecting of the Church. But it is not reason thus to confound Christ with His Church. Christ and the Church are not convertible terms. It is not the same thing to seek the manifestation of Christ in the growth of the Church, and to seek the growth of the Church. In the one case "Christ," in the other "the Church" occupies the centre of thought; and the effect of that difference upon all missionary work is most profound and far-reaching.[12]

Not Focused on Social Improvement

Not only was Allen concerned with missionaries who placed their focus on converts and church growth but he also had a concern with a priority on social improvement. Concerning this danger, Allen warned:

> There is a strong tendency to-day towards propagating social theories which seem to us Christian, towards making the progress of the world our hope. Men see the truth in heathen religions, they see the virtues of heathen character and they urge that the end of Christian missionary work is

> not so much to convert individual, not so much to establish the Church, as to leaven society and to help forward a movement towards a goal of glory to which heathen truth and Christian truth alike are tending. . . . The result is that they would make missionaries, preachers of social and political righteousness more than preachers of Christ.[13]

The necessary element to prevent this shifting of the missionary focus to social reform was the revelation of Christ.

> But if we habitually speak and think of the Revelation of Christ as the end, if it is the Person of Christ that we desire above all things, we cannot rest in social perfection, we cannot set a false end before us, we cannot degenerate into social reformers.[14]

In summary, how do we reconcile Allen's previous statement "May I, then, take it as agreed that evangelization is the supreme end of missions?" with the idea that the focus is to be on the revelation of Christ as the utmost priority? The answer is not as difficult as it may appear. First, Allen's comments regarding the revelation of Christ appeared seven years prior to his article "The Relation between Medical, Educational and Evangelistic Work in Foreign Missions." His understanding of the proper focus had already been established. For Allen, the revelation of Christ was evangelism.

Second, just as the apostolic church had received the Spirit which moved them to take the gospel of salvation to all the world, Allen understood that contemporary missionaries had received the same Spirit with the same global purpose. The priority of evangelism had not changed. Just as the apostles had the attitude that they could not stop speaking about what they had seen and heard (Acts 4:20), Allen assumed that contemporary missionaries were to have the same attitude.

Making disciples was still to be the priority (Matt 28:19-20), but was not the focus; lost men and women were not the focus. Christ was the focus. Missionaries could keep everything in the proper perspective only when they focused on revealing Christ to the lost. Because the lost were chosen "in Him before the foundation of the world" (Eph 1:4), the missionary was responsible for making Christ known so that others might believe. As it is written:

> How then will they call on him in whom they have not believed? And how are they to believe in him of whom they have never heard? And how are they to hear without someone preaching? (Rom 10:14)

When the missionary understood that the focus was to reveal Christ by proclaiming the good news, secondary issues such as conversions, church extension, and social reformation would fall into proper perspective as Christ transformed people's lives.

Apostolic Approach

Having noted that in just over ten years the apostle Paul was able to establish the Church in four provinces of the Empire, Allen made a contrast to his own day:

> This is truly an astonishing fact. That churches should be founded as rapidly, so securely, seems to us today, accustomed to the difficulties, the uncertainties, the failures, the disastrous relapses of our own missionary work, almost incredible. Many missionaries in later days have received a larger number of converts than St. Paul; many have preached over a wider area than he; but none have so established churches. We have forgotten that such things could be. We have long accustomed ourselves to accept it as an axiom of missionary work that converts in a new country must be submitted to a very long probation and training, extending over generations before they can be expected to be able to stand alone. Today if a man ventures to suggest that there may be something in the methods by which St. Paul attained such wonderful results worthy of our careful attention, and perhaps of our imitation, he is in danger of being accused of revolutionary tendencies.[15]

Allen firmly believed that Luke recorded the accounts of Paul not for mere "archaeological and historical interest," but rather, "like the rest of the Holy Scriptures it was 'written for our learning.'"[16]

Allen was convinced that the apostle Paul passed along four critical elements to the new believers that were essential for them to exist as a church: the Creed, the Sacraments, the Orders, and the Holy Scriptures.[17] What Allen referred to as the Creed was actually not a formal creed at all, but rather a teaching containing the "simple Gospel" involving a doctrine of God the Father, the Creator; a doctrine of Jesus, the Son, the Redeemer, the Savior; and a doctrine of the Holy Spirit, the indwelling source of strength. In conjunction with these teachings was the reliance on an oral tradition of the fundamental facts behind the death and resurrection of Christ.[18]

The Sacraments were also passed along to the new church. Paul educated the believers regarding the manner and significance behind the Lord's Supper and baptism. According to Allen, these were not optional for any congregation Paul founded. In Paul's writings, it was taken for granted that all believers had been baptized and met regularly for communion.[19] The requirements for baptism were repentance and faith. "The moment a man showed that he had repentance and faith, he was baptized into Christ Jesus, in order that Christ in him might perfect that repentance and faith, and bring it to its full end, holiness in the Body of Christ."[20]

The Orders referred to the leaders. Paul made sure that the new believers had elders overseeing them. Allen stated that "just as he [Paul] baptized three or four and then committed the responsibility for admitting others to those whom he had baptized; so he ordained three or four and committed the authority for ordaining others into their hands."[21] Paul's selection of elders *from the church* instead of outside of the church was extremely important in the interpersonal relationships that would exist between the elders and the church as a whole. Concerning this relational bond, Allen explained:

> This is of the utmost importance. It makes a great difference if the ministers feel some responsibility to those to whom they minister, and if the general congregation feels some responsibility for the character and work of those who are set over them. Where candidates for the ministry are selected by the superior order, where they are ordained solely on the authority of the superior order, and are appointed to their posts by the sole direction of the superior order, those who are so appointed are apt to lose any sense of responsibility to the congregation among whom they minister, and the congregation feels no responsibility for them. The result is an inevitable weakening of what should be the strongest support, both to clergy and laity. Where the superior order consists almost wholly of foreigners, the result is often deplorable.[22]

The final element that the apostle Paul passed along to the new congregation was the Holy Scriptures. Paul taught the believers the importance of the Old Testament writings. Paul lectured from the Old Testament and some learned how to "read the Old Testament and to read it in a mystic sense as applying to Gentile Christians. . . . Anyone who had been reading the book and had discovered a passage which seemed to point to Christ, or an exhortation which seemed applicable to the circumstances of their life, or a promise which encouraged him with hope for this life or the next, produced it and explained it for the benefit of all."[23]

In Allen's thought, these were the four necessities that the apostle Paul passed on to each of the churches he started: the Creed, the Sacraments, the Orders, and the Holy Scriptures. Before the apostle could retire (i.e., move on to plant other churches), one last practice had to occur before the new church could be able to fully grasp the four necessities that had been passed on to them. The apostle had to practice the ministration of the Spirit.[24] But before this practice can be addressed, it is necessary to understand a common missionary paradigm of Allen's day—devolution.

---

[1] Arthur P. Johnston, *The Battle for World Evangelism* (Wheaton, IL: Tyndale House Publishers, 1978), 33, 59.

[2] Roland Allen, "The Relation Between Medical, Educational and Evangelistic Work in Foreign Missions," *Church Missionary Society* (March 1920): 57.

[3] Ibid., 58.

[4] Roland Allen, *Missionary Principles* (Grand Rapids, MI: William B. Eerdmans, 1964), 67.

[5] Ibid., 68.

[6] Ibid., 73-74.

[7] Ibid., 84.

[8] Ibid., 85.

[9] Ibid., 86.

[10] Ibid., 90.

[11] Ibid.

[12] Ibid., 93.

[13] Ibid., 95-96.

[14] Ibid., 97.

[15] Roland Allen, *Missionary Methods: St. Paul's or Ours?*, American ed. (Grand Rapids, MI: Wm. B. Eerdmans, 1962), 3-4.

[16] Ibid., 4. Throughout Allen's life, he encountered many rebuttals to his belief that the apostolic pattern was relevant for any day. Allen spent time countering these rebuttals and many of his writings were polemical in nature. It is beyond the scope of this book to address the rebuttals and Allen's responses. For further information regarding these issues see the introduction to *Missionary Methods: St. Paul's or Ours?* and *Educational Principles and Missionary Methods.*

[17] Roland Allen, *Missionary Methods: St. Paul's or Ours?*, American ed. (Grand Rapids, MI: Wm. B. Eerdmans, 1962), 107.

[18] Ibid., 87-88.

[19] Ibid., 89.

[20] Ibid., 97.

[21] Ibid., 100. Allen based his understanding of only baptizing a few and then turning the responsibility over to the church from 1 Cor 1:14-17: "I thank God that I baptized none of you except Crispus and Gaius, so that no one would say you were baptized in my name. Now I did baptize also the household of Stephanas; beyond that, I do not know whether I baptized any other. For Christ did not send me to baptize, but to preach the gospel, not in cleverness of speech, so that the cross of Christ would not be made void." See Roland Allen, "The Essentials of an Indigenous Church," *The Chinese Recorder* 56 (1925): 493.

[22] Ibid., 100-01.

[23] Ibid., 88-89.

[24] This practice reveals an example of the integration of Allen's missiology, thus displaying the difficulty in an attempt to systematize it. Here the apostle must pass on to the new believers the Creed, Sacraments, Orders, and Holy Scriptures; however, without the ministration of the Spirit, this was an impossible task. In other words, while the apostle was passing on the four necessities described above, he was simultaneously ministering the Spirit.

Chapter 7
Devolution

In 1927, Allen published an article entitled "Devolution: The Question of the Hour," in which he critiqued the common practice. He argued that the origin and meaning of the word *devolution* was derived from a governmental practice involving the delegation of authority. Quoting the *New English Dictionary*, he stated that devolution meant "'the delegation or leaving of portions or details of duties to subordinate officers or committees'; 'the passing of power or authority from one person or body to another.'"[1] When applied to missionary practice, devolution was the approach that gradually delegated rights and privileges to a local congregation. Holding to this practice meant that a new congregation was viewed as not being capable of functioning as a mature congregation. The missionary, therefore, had to oversee the community until the believers could stand on their own without external aid; this oversight included granting authority to the congregation from the missionary or mission agency.

Three Questions

In this article Allen sought to answer three questions. First, did a mission have any authority to which it could delegate to a congregation? Second, what was the nature of the authority that a mission claimed? Third, what was the understanding of a church to the mission which practiced devolution?

In response to the first question, Allen emphatically stated that the devolution as found in the New Testament is not the same as that practiced by contemporary missionaries. For Allen, the contemporary concept had absolutely no place in the Scriptures.

> St. Paul, for instance, established a Church when he organized converts with their own proper officers, but he did not organize a Church and then later, and piece by piece, devolve an authority which at first the Church did not possess. He devolved all necessary power and authority upon the Church when he established it. . . . When St. Paul had once established a Church there was nothing left to devolve. We read nowhere of his going back to a Church and adding to its powers by devolving upon it some responsibility or authority which he had before kept in his own hands.[2]

Allen did not believe that the mission agencies had any authority that could be delegated to the new congregations. Apart from the missionaries passing along the Creed, Sacraments, Orders, and Holy Scriptures to the established congregation, nothing else was to be devolved.

Allen anticipated that some would respond to his critique of devolution by stating that his comments were irrelevant because missions did not claim spiritual authority over new churches, but rather earthly authority related to funding, location of agents, and the passing of bylaws.[3] It was to this earthly authority that Allen attempted to address the second question: What was the nature of the authority for which a mission made claim? This authority was based on three areas: (1) control of funds, (2) responsibility for evangelization, and (3) responsibility for the care of churches.

Allen understood the control of funds as the most discussed topic among these three areas.[4]

> If the indigenous Church is to appear by a process of devolution, as we are told, it is a matter worthy of serious concern that money should be put into this place; for it means that the indigenous Church is to appear when it has control of funds, and that unless it can obtain control of funds, the Church cannot be indigenous. For me, simply to write that down is to refute it; but since it seems to be almost universally accepted as an axiom, since our ideas of a Church are bound up apparently with paid ministers, and our ideas of evangelization with paid evangelists, and our ideas of Christian education with costly institutions, I suppose that I must attempt to say something more. . . . To confuse the Church with a financial Committee is not far from blasphemy. The Church is not the Temple of Mammon, but of the Holy Ghost.[5]

Allen addressed this issue of the control of funds in the third section of the article, which discussed the concept of the Church. The above quote, however, revealed his disdain for equating the control of foreign monies with the indigenous concept and foreshadowed his austere rebuke yet to follow.

Allen was also concerned about missions devolving the responsibility for evangelism to the native church. Concerning this aspect of devolution, he emphasized that "responsibility for evangelization is the responsibility of the possessors of Truth to hand it on. It is a spiritual responsibility which rests upon the Church and upon every member of the Church."[6] This responsibility cannot be delegated. It is a responsibility that has been mandated by the Lord and not to be derived from a mission agency or missionary.

Again, Allen anticipated a rebuttal to his comments. He agreed that some might say that when a mission spoke of devolving the responsibility for evangelism, it was not referring to the biblical mandate, but rather the right to control the funds necessary to support the evangelistic work (i.e., evangelists).[7] To this declaration, Allen responded by noting that missionaries had placed evangelism into a materialistic category.

> It means that we ourselves have so learnt to look upon evangelization as a matter of money and paid agents, that we have taught our converts to look upon it in that light. Evangelization has been removed out of the sphere of spiritual and moral obligation into the sphere of the

> material and the commercial, and consequently can be treated as a matter for devolution. But every time we deny that our devolution has anything to do with spiritual authority, we deny that it has anything essentially to do with the establishment of a spiritual Church.[8]

The final area of authority that was to be devolved was the responsibility for the care of the churches. In Allen's day, the practice of transferring the church from the watch care of the mission to the auspices of the national Church was commonplace. He believed this process to be an unnecessary and superfluous act. He questioned how the local church could become the church when the mission declared her as such.

Allen viewed this philosophy of devolving the care of the churches to the national Church as fostering codependency and proclaiming that the mission originally had ownership of the converts and churches. He wrote:

> To transfer a Church to the Church implies and demands that before its transference it was a dependency of something other than the Church; and that is very strange. All this language springs from a conception of missionary work which implies that converts are the property of the Mission through which they were converted. Converts are made and become in the making under the government of the Mission, and then can be treated as under that

> Government and transferred, or not transferred, to another Government.[9]

In answer to the second question, regarding the nature of the authority claimed, according to tradition the mission did have authority to delegate to the national Church. This authority, however, was based on a paradigm that was not from the Scriptures. This paradigm distorted the biblical responsibilities and authority that already belonged to the national Church by divine mandate. What the churches already possessed was barred from their use. The authority that was declared to be the right of the mission agency had a spiritual façade covering a humanistic core.

The final question Allen addressed in this article was, "What was the understanding of the Church to the mission agency which practiced devolution?" Prior to explaining his answer, he established his understanding of the church:

> In the New Testament the idea of a Church is simple. It is an organized body of Christians in a place with its officers. The Christians with their officers are the Church in the place, and they are addressed as such. That is simple and intelligible. That Church is the visible Body of Christ in the place, and it has all the rights and privileges and duties of the Body of Christ. Above it is the Universal Church, composed of all the Churches in the world, and of all the redeemed in heaven and on earth. The Apostolic idea of

> the Church is wonderfully intelligible to men everywhere… .The Apostolic system is so simple, that it can be apprehended by men in every stage of education, and civilization.[10]

The missionary paradigm that fostered devolution was a complex system. How could any people (i.e., Easterners), without devolution, maintain the ecclesiastical system that took highly educated Westerners years to develop and apply? Without proper education and experiential training, it was impossible for a new congregation to continue with the foreign Church infrastructure.

Allen noted that the understanding of Church behind the concept of devolution was the idea of "the Church as a Committee." The mission "represented by a Committee devolves its authority over Christians to a Committee which it calls the Native Church because its members are Native Christians, or Native Christians are in the majority."[11] He further stated: "I think that I am safe in saying that the idea of a Committee is always prominent, and the indigenous Church is to appear either when the Committee is composed wholly of Natives of the country, or when Natives are in a majority on the Committee, and that the Committee represents the Church and is spoken of as the Church for the purposes of devolution" (see Figure 2).

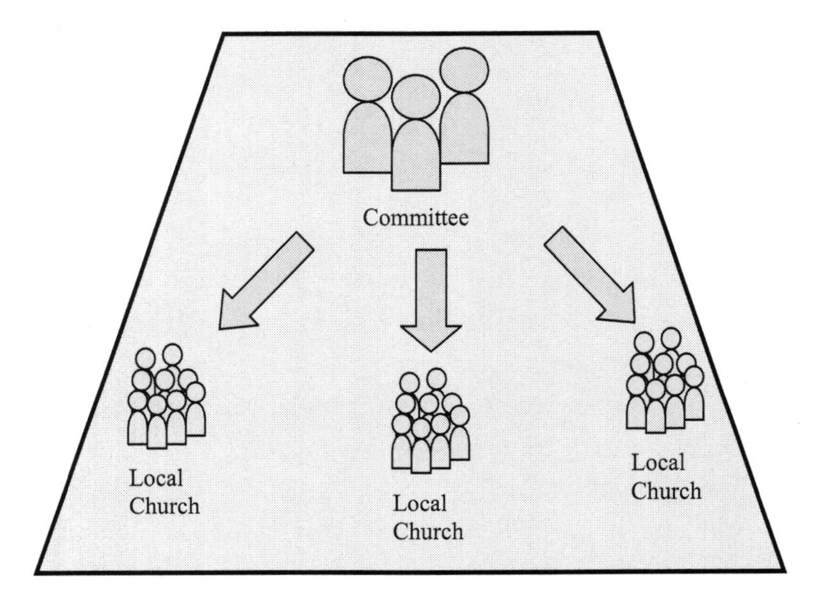

Figure 2. Devolution

In the article, Allen never fully developed this description of the Church being a committee. He did, however, assert the following:

> The Committee is supposed to represent the Church, or to be the Church; but even if it could truly be said to represent the Church, it certainly is not representative of the Church. It is generally a body composed of ex-officio members and members who in some way are elected by, or sent from, self-supporting Churches (*i.e.*, congregations rich enough to pay a minister); it, therefore, is

> representative only of the richer and more highly educated element of the Christian population. Its business is largely financial, and when not directly financial, depends upon a financial basis; it, therefore, keeps the financial side of Church life in the foreground. Its activities are incomprehensible to the great mass of the less educated laity, who know little of them and understand less. It passes resolutions and transacts business for the Church over the heads of the great majority of the Christians. Most of the members of the Church live all their days in local congregations which are not Churches and have no proper Church organization, and are mere dependents upon this Committee and its Agents. In this way it robs the majority of the Christians of any true knowledge of what the Church is.[12]

Allen viewed devolution as a serious threat to the spontaneous expansion of the Church. For him, devolution contained two serious problems. First, "it proclaims that the Mission is first lord over the Church of God, with authority to give or to withhold the ordinary rights of the Christians at its will."[13] In even more poignant words, he emphasized that devolution "sets up a Committee in the place of Christ and offers the Committee authority to control the Church regardless of the right of the local Churches to their own proper Church life."[14]

The second major problem of devolution was that "it inverts the whole order of Christ. It teaches men to look forward to attaining what they ought to have at the very beginning."[15] In the concluding section of his article, Allen remarked:

> The answer is simple: the Church with which devolution is concerned is not the Church as St. Paul conceived it or established it. Devolution has no place in his conception of the Church. Christ came first. Spiritual power came first. The establishment of the Body of Christ came first.[16]

Yet, even in light of the longstanding practice of devolution, Allen understood that there was a more excellent way.

---

[1] Roland Allen, "Devolution: The Question of the Hour," *World Dominion* 5 (1927): 276.

[2] Ibid., 278.

[3] Ibid., 279.

[4] Ibid., 280.

[5] Ibid.

[6] Ibid., 281.

[7] Ibid., 281-82.

[8] Ibid., 282.

[9] Ibid.

[10] Ibid., 283-84.

[11] Ibid., 283.

[12] Ibid., 285.

[13] Ibid., 286.

[14] Ibid.

[15] Ibid., 287.

[16] Ibid.

Chapter 8
Missionary Faith

Encompassing all the missionary priorities was missionary faith (see Figure 1). This faith was not a salvific faith nor was it related to having faith in God that He would bring people to repentance. This faith was rather a faith in the Spirit's ability to sustain His churches, without the missionary's domination and without devolution. Because the new churches had the Holy Spirit indwelling them and because the missionaries had passed along the Creed, Sacraments, Orders, and Holy Scriptures, the churches could stand on their own.

In Allen's article "The Place of 'Faith' in Missionary Evangelism" (1930), he contrasted the missionary approach of Christians with the propagation approaches of adherents to other religions. The results were startling. Allen saw that Muslims and Buddhists were closer to the apostolic approach of Paul than many Christian missionaries. Concerning Islam in China, he observed:

> But where they [Muslim missionaries] went with a doctrine which they sincerely believed they made converts. Mosques sprang up. The doctrine which they taught was given wholly to the Chinese. . . . From father to son, from neighbour to neighbour, from friend to friend the doctrine was taught, and the rites, and those who received them were expected naturally to practice them and to hand them

> on. . . . No precautions were taken to secure its purity, no institutions, which the Chinese Moslems did not themselves create, were raised to train its leaders, or to attract converts: *everything* was rooted in the conviction that the doctrine was so good that it could be entrusted to *anybody.*[1]

Regarding the early Buddhists missionaries in China, Allen wrote:

> They certainly had a great faith in the doctrine which they taught. Manifestly they were so persuaded that their doctrine and the rites in which it was expressed were so good that these precious gifts could be given to anybody who would receive them without fear; and that those who received them would be so impressed by them that they would not only hold them but hand them on to others. . . . The monasteries were ruled by Chinese, the rites were preformed by Chinese, the doctrine was taught by Chinese.[2]

Despite the threat of corruption and opposition, which did take place from time to time, the Muslims and Buddhists in China continued to practice a catalytic approach, having faith in the power behind their false teachings. It was this type of faith that Allen believed was among Christian missionaries. Writing of those Christian missionaries, he argued:

> They do not *so* believe the doctrine which they preach; they cannot *so* entrust the doctrine and the rites to others. . . . The fact is that our missionaries cannot, or will not, entrust the doctrine and the rites of the Christian faith to raw converts, in the simple faith that the Gospel can stand in its own strength. They act as if they thought that the religion which they preach could not stand in its own strength.[3]

It was this lack of faith that hindered the spontaneous expansion of the Church.

Allen hypothesized that the major reason that missionaries were not willing to trust the new believers was because of fear of corruption and degeneration among the churches. What happens if false teachers come along? What will the result be if division strikes the church? Who will the new believers turn to for help in making the proper decisions? Allen realized that just as Paul's churches experienced problems, contemporary churches would do likewise. Despite this reality, Allen firmly held to the apostolic pattern.[4] The arguments that foretold of all the possible evil that men and women could bring to a church "admit that we do not believe that our Gospel is so powerful that it can of itself raise a fallen race."[5]

Allen believed that Christ was able to keep new churches from stumbling (Jude 24). In order for the missionaries to be able to have the proper faith, a paradigm shift was in order.

> We fear corruption and degeneration; when shall we cease to fear them? The roots of that fear are in us, and when shall we eradicate them, and how? There will always be cause for that fear, if we look at men. If we look at Christ then we may escape; but then why should we not escape now? He does not change. When we talk of a day when we shall be able to trust our converts in non-Christian lands, we are looking at them. So long as we look at them we shall be afraid.[6]

Allen realized that contemporary missionaries were practicing not only an anthropocentric focus to missions but they were very also very ethnocentric in their views of when a church could stand on its own. He believed that missionaries were measuring the spiritual maturity of the new churches by their own spiritual maturity. In essence, they were advocating, "When the new churches arrive at our level, then they can be on their own." Of the various problems related to ethnocentric mission work, Allen mentioned the following in the article:

> They suggest that *we* are fit to be entrusted with the Gospel, and that when others are as we are they will be fit; but that is a most unjustifiable assumption. It is utterly untrue, manifestly untrue. We are not entrusted with the Gospel because we are righteous, and have attained some standard of intelligence and morality, but because God has had mercy on us. Not for our righteousness, but

according to His lovingkindness, He has chosen us; and we stand by faith.[7]

Proper missionary faith was the bond that held together the various responsibilities of the missionary. Without a christocentric focus and reliance on the power of the gospel and the Sprit, devolution was the solution. Until a healthy faith manifested itself in the lives and practices of the missionaries, there could be no priority of evangelism, apostolic approach, and the ministration of the Spirit. Without a healthy faith, ultimately, there could be no spontaneous expansion of the Church.

---

[1] Ibid., 236-37. For more information on the Islamic paradigm, see Roland Allen, "Islam and Christianity in the Sudan," *The International Review of Missions* 9 (1920): 531-43; and Roland Allen, "Brotherhood: A Contrast Between Moslem Practice and Christian Ideals," *World Dominion* 1 (1923): 92-94.

[2] Roland Allen, "The Place of 'Faith' in Missionary Evangelism," *World Dominion* 8 (1930): 235.

[3] Ibid., 237.

[4] In *Missionary Methods: St. Paul's or Ours?*, Allen wrote: "Now if we are to practise any methods approaching to the Pauline methods in power and directness, it is absolutely necessary that we should first have this faith, this Spirit. Without faith—faith in the Holy Ghost, faith in the Holy Ghost in our converts—we can do nothing. We cannot possibly act as the Apostle acted until we recover this faith" (152).

[5] Allen, "The Place of 'Faith' in Missionary Evangelism," 240.

[6] Ibid., 238.

[7] Ibid., 240.

Chapter 9
Leadership Development

Not only was Allen focused on the Spirit as the one who moved the Church to mission but he was also concerned about the influence of the missionary on the inhabitants of any given country. Contemporary methodologies erected unnecessary barriers between the converts and the Spirit's work, thus hindering the development of leaders.

> Do we not talk of creating leaders *by* training? What are we saying? We are saying that the means employed produce the effect. We say that our training makes leaders, our education enlightens the intellect, our social work ameliorates conditions of life. Well, suppose they do: these are not the ends which we set before ourselves: the end which we set before ourselves was a revelation of the power of the Holy Ghost. We have either lost sight of the end or we have put the means, our "activities," into His place. When the activities usurp the place of the Holy Spirit, the Spirit is obscured and hidden, because He is in fact deposed from His rightful place. It is He who creates leaders, it is He who enlightens, it is He who uplifts, it is He who teaches men to "live," whatever the conditions in which they live. We cannot have it both ways.[1]

The infatuation of the missionaries with this anthropocentric methodology for leadership development was a concern that consumed much of Allen's thought. According to Michael Don Thompson, "He saw the Spirit as empowering the entire mission of the Church, converting sinners and establishing them in their new faith, calling forth leaders from among the new converts, and guiding infant churches to maturity."[2]

Native Education

Allen's views on native education were closely connected with his understanding of indigenous churches. The common missionary practice of his day was the importation of Western pedagogical systems into non-Western contexts. It was assumed that what worked well in Western Christian education and theological education would suffice elsewhere. This methodology fostered a dependency on external resources for church education. It should also be noted that this common methodology was training and equipping the people to maintain the foreign systems and organizations, which were imported by the missionaries.[3]

For Allen, native education was to develop out of the indigenous Church in a given region.

> If Christian education ought to be in the Church, of the Church, and by the Church . . . then it must begin with the foundation of the Church at the very beginning. . . . If the Church is established as soon as there are Christians in any place, a Church in the Biblical sense endowed with all the responsibilities and duties and rights and authority

> essential to the existence of a Church, Christian education begins at its very foundation and grows with the growth of the Church.[4]

Though the educational systems created by missionaries were established to train Church leaders, as time progressed the missionaries realized that the schools could serve other purposes, such as educating nonbelievers. The imported institutions were costly and "by admitting the children of non-Christians who desired education in the arts and sciences, the founders of these institutions received fees and sometimes government grants which assisted considerably in their maintenance, whilst at the same time they hoped to influence and even convert some of the students who might be expected in later years to occupy positions of influence in the country."[5] Overall, four very serious problems encompassed this approach to education.

First, a dichotomy occurred between the education of the Church leaders and the Church itself. This dichotomy separated both the educational institutions and the Church leaders from the local churches. Allen noted that "leaders were selected for the Church by foreigners and they were educated in institutions founded by foreigners and maintained by foreigners, for which the native Christians as a body had no responsibility."[6] This separation disconnected the institutions and leaders-to-be from the real concerns and needs at the local level. The following quote by Allen revealed the anthropocentric nature of the educational process. Referring to the national leaders, he stated:

> They were not trained because they were leaders in the Church, and the Church wanted them trained; they were trained because foreigners wanted to train them in their own way in the hope that they would assist them in their work. They were trained nominally for the Church, but not by the Church nor in the Church and when they were trained, if they led at all, they were far more leaders in the mission organization than in the Church. In relation to the Native Church they were often almost as foreign as the foreign missionaries.[7]

A second problem that Allen saw was related to a dichotomy between the Christian education and the native life. The educational process was grounded in Western structure and pedagogy and out of touch with the culture around it. In cultures where the national government had established an educational system, the Christian institutions many times had been viewed as useless to life within the particular culture. Allen commented that "the Government has its own system of education side by side with the mission system, and, beyond recognizing mission institutions and supporting them with grants in aid, has no responsibility for their continued existence. Governments indeed tend rather to restrict the religious teaching given in them by adopting conscience clauses, which they enforce by threatening to withdraw the grants in aid."[8] In many cases the government programs did a much better job at educating its own people than the foreign missionaries ever accomplished.

A third problem that Allen noticed about the missionary's approach to native education was that over time the original purpose for the education changed. This shifting of purpose resulted in the churches not understanding the educational system. In the beginning, the founders desired that the education imported was for the purpose of educating leaders for the native Church. As time progressed, the purpose of Christian education shifted completely to a variety of issues: focusing on the evangelization of nonbelievers, improving the country socially and morally, and influencing the people's minds in preparation for the gospel message.[9]

Because of this distorted purpose for Christian education, Allen observed:

> The Native Christians themselves do not know what the institutions are founded for. They often say that they are not founded specifically and definitely for them, and as I have said they feel no responsibility for them. . . . The system is incomprehensible to the natives. They are full of trust in some excellent heads of institutions whom they know, but full of distrust of the system which they cannot comprehend.[10]

A final weakness that Allen saw in the contemporary mission approach to Christian education on the field was that the institutions that admitted large numbers of nonbelievers and did not convert them were educating some opponents to the

Christian faith.[11] In his thoughts, though the institutions may have had good intentions, they were actually doing harm in many cases.

---

[1] Roland Allen, *Mission Activities Considered in Relation to the Manifestation of the Spirit* (London: World Dominion Press, 1927), 13-14.

[2] Michael Don Thompson, "The Holy Spirit and Human Instrumentality in the Training of New Converts: An Evaluation of the Missiological Thought of Roland Allen" (Ph.D. diss., Golden Gate Baptist Theological Seminary, 1989), 51.

[3] Roland Allen, "The Native Church and Mission Education," *World Dominion* 3 (1925): 154.

[4] Roland Allen, "Education in the Native Church," *World Dominion* 4 (1925): 37.

[5] Allen, "The Native Church and Mission Education," 154.

[6] Ibid., 155.

[7] Ibid.

[8] Ibid., 156.

[9] Ibid., 156, 157.

[10] Ibid., 157.

[11] Ibid.

Chapter 10
Voluntary Clergy[1]

Because missionaries received a stipend from the missionary societies, they could not help but propagate the same stipendiary system on the mission field. According to Allen, the missionaries "soon began to train natives to work with them, as evangelists and teachers and pastors, and they paid them. Thus very early the native Christian community was divided into two classes, workers who were called mission agents, and the rest who were not."[2] Though the mission agents were initially supported by the mission, as time progressed the national people were urged to support the mission agents. Thus the concept of self-support came to refer to a group who could provide the "maintenance of buildings and the supply of stipends."[3] Allen observed the prominence of this belief:

> It is hardly too much to say that often the duty of supporting paid workers has become one of the first lessons, if not the very first lesson, given to inquirers. That lesson may not be taught verbally by direct assertion; but it is taught by a demand that they must provide and maintain a building and support a teacher if they are to be admitted to the Christian fold; and when once they are within it is taught as a Christian duty of the first importance. Evangelists, teachers, and pastors must all be supported, and it is the duty of the laity to support them.[4]

Allen argued against the belief that ordained men must be limited to those not involved in any secular livelihood. He stressed that a stipend was not necessary for a clergyman to be present: "What is quite clear is that in the Apostolic age the establishment of a Church with its proper ministers did not depend at all upon the provision of a stipend which might set the ministers free from common toil; it had nothing to do with a banker's account. The Apostles and their successors did ordain men regardless of stipends: that is all that needs to be proved."[5]

There are at least fourteen particular problems that Allen believed were related to importing a stipendiary system onto newly established churches. The first problem with the system was that it denied churches the Lord's Supper and baptism. This problem was one which consumed much of Allen's thought and revealed just how far the Church had deviated from the biblical indigenous church concept.

According to Allen, the common philosophy within the Anglican Church of his day was if the congregations did not have a minister, they were not a legitimate congregation and could not practice the rites. To have a minister required a stipendiary system for the financial assistance of the particular clergyman. If the money was not available, the congregation did not receive their own ordained clergy; since the ordained could only administer the Lord's Supper, the church went without the ordinance. Allen summarized this rule with the phrase "No stipends no clergy."[6]

A second problem with the stipendiary system was that it

established a "missions by proxy" approach. Allen thought that the stipendiary system was a poor model for the new believers. He wrote that the approach teaches "all our converts that it is the duty of Christians to evangelize by paying evangelists."[7]

A third problem, which was closely related to the second, was that a stipendiary system posed a poor witness of the community of believers and of the gospel itself. Allen believed that in the eyes of society, the system displayed a religion without power. Referring to the viewpoints of non-Westerners, he reflected:

> Our organization seems to them to put the wrong things first. We collect money and pay men to preach and teach. Outside our circle nearly all men think that very strange. All knowledge, above all, religious knowledge, is a divine gift and to connect it with money is a sort of simony. A paid preacher is suspected as a preacher paid to teach what he is told to teach by those who pay him; not the inspired possessor of a divine gift.
>
> An organization which collects money and pays salaries to missionaries of a divine faith seems to such men a monstrous thing, wholly unspiritual.[8]

Allen also realized that when a church leader from a new congregation was receiving financial compensation for preaching the gospel, the people of the region would view the individual as a hireling.

> If he is a paid agent both speaker and hearer are affected by that fact. The speaker knows, and knows that the other knows, that he is employed by a mission to speak. He is not delivering his own message because he cannot help it. He is not speaking of Christ because Christ alone impels him. Do men not ask our paid agents: "How much are you paid for this work?" And must they not answer? And does not the answer destroy the effect of which we have been thinking?[9]

A disclaimer related to this third problem must be included. Allen was not opposed to paid clergy. In an almost contradictory fashion, he devoted the beginning of chapter five in *The Case for Voluntary Clergy* to explaining the need for a stipendiary clergy. He did not explain the conundrum he established there. He did, however, comment that there are individuals like Socrates and the apostle Paul who refused to receive any compensation for religious service. As long as the position of the clergy was equated with a stipend, people such as these will never accept the office.[10] Within this chapter, he stressed:

> We ought not to oppose them [stipendiary and voluntary clergy] as if one excluded the other. It must be plain to any one who has read my chapter on the Apostolic qualifications that I did not there attempt to prove that the clergy should never be paid. The Apostolic qualifications

> are quite compatible with dependence for livelihood upon the offerings of the faithful, either in the form of endowments, or of subscriptions. The means by which the minister gains his living is not in the picture. He may earn it by a trade, or inherit wealth from his ancestors, or enjoy a salary, or receive dues as an official, or be supported by the Church. How he is supported is a mere external detail, which is not even mentioned. His call of God and his service do not depend upon such things as that. The Church unquestionably needs some men who give themselves wholly to prayer and the ministration of the Word and Sacraments, and such men must be supported by the faithful.[11]

This apparent contradiction is alleviated when we understand that Allen was not opposed to paying itinerant clergy. His opposition was against paying a stipend to established overseers of a local congregation. Allen noted that the qualifications for the ministry found in the Pastoral Epistles did not include anything that necessitated the resigning of the minister from his original livelihood so he could pastor a church. Allen wrote that "such silence rather suggests that the man will continue to live his life as he has been living it and providing for his family as he has been providing for it."[12] Allen continued:

> It is said that those who spend all their time as itinerant preachers might rightly expect support at the hand of the

> faithful. . . . But those passages [1 Cor 9:1-14; Luke 10:7; Matt 10:10] do not refer to the settled presbyters or bishops of whom the Apostle is writing to Timothy and Titus. . . . But it would require much ingenuity and imagination to read into these passages [Gal 6:6; 1 Tim 5:17] any suggestion that the ordinance of the Lord and the Apostolic exhortations to the faithful involved the conclusion that all the presbyters, or even all the travelling evangelists, necessarily must depend entirely upon the alms of the laity.[13]

In all of Allen's missiology, his understanding of who should receive compensation and who should not receive compensation is possibly the most difficult concept to understand. Even within the same publication, at times he seems to contradict himself. The majority of Allen's writings concerning voluntary clergy are opposed to a stipendiary system. It is quotes such as those cited above that confuse the reader.[14]

A fourth problem that the stipendiary system caused was that it prevented the local congregation from experiencing the ministry that rightly belonged to it. When churches were established in the New Testament, the focus was on the local bodies of Christ in a given area, not on the clergy. Allen believed that tradition had resulted in the establishment not of the Church but of the "clergy as a class apart, and of ordination not as the establishment of the Church but as the admission of selected individuals to membership in a professional order."[15]

His fifth concern with the stipendiary system was that it fostered unbiblical qualifications for the clergy. For a man to be a clergyman and thus receive a stipend, he had to meet the necessary qualifications as established by the Church. Allen, however, believed these contemporary qualifications for the ministry deviated greatly from that of the apostolic qualifications established in the Scriptures.[16] These contemporary qualifications prevented many qualified individuals from the ministry and placed unqualified individuals into places of leadership.

A sixth problem with the stipendiary system was that it delayed the organization of a local church. Because in the early days of a church there were no qualified leaders, he commented that "thus the organization of the Church is delayed in a most unhealthy way, and the clerical order is established on a most unhealthy basis, whilst the natural leaders of the Christian people are suppressed, and put into a very false position."[17] The solution to the problem was that the missionaries should ordain voluntary clergy.

A seventh problem was that it was difficult for stipendiary clergy to be a true part of the lives of the people.

> Among our own people also the church sorely needs clergy in close touch with the ordinary life of the laity, living the life of ordinary men, sharing their difficulties and understanding their trials by close personal experience. Stipendiary clergy cut off by training and life from that common experience are constantly struggling to get close

> to the laity by wearing lay clothing, sharing in lay amusements, and organizing lay clubs; but they never quite succeed. To get close to men, it is necessary really to share their experience, and to share their experience is to share it by being in it, not merely to come as near to it as possible without being in it. The church needs clerics who really share the life of their people. The life of the voluntary cleric is not divorced from the life of the laity, it is the life of the laity lived as a cleric ought to live it.[18]

Because the stipendiary system created a class of clergy separated from the rest of the local congregation, the ministers were not as close to the people as Allen desired. Training and education erected unnecessary barriers among the people.

An eighth problem was that it fostered a dependency mentality on finances. The people had become dependant on the Western concept of a necessary stipend for a minister. Allen warned against this practice of establishing the Church on a financial foundation.

> If we begin by making the establishment of the Church in a new place dependent upon the maintenance of stipendiary clergy and possibly, often, or rather generally, upon the supply of a building, I do not see how the conclusion can be avoided. There can be no Church in a place until money is forthcoming for the stipend of the cleric and the erection and maintenance of the building. The clergy must be supported, and if the clergy are not

> permitted to support themselves by any trade or profession, the laity must support them; and if the laity are to support them, the laity must be urged to support them, and before clergy can be ordained the laity must produce the funds.
>
> The money must come first in time. But it is certain that what is put first in time tends to be put first in thought. It usurps the first place in the mind, because it is the immediate pressing need.[19]

A ninth concern with the system was that it created a graduated pay scale that paid some people greater stipends than others. Those of the higher ministry orders received more pay than those of the lower orders. The result was that an increase in pay reflected progress in Christian service. In Allen's words "The pay grades the man."[20]

A tenth problem with the stipendiary system was related to the impression of the Mission holding the finances. When the indigenous people saw the money coming from the Westerners, there was the tendency for them to work for the Mission rather than for Christ. Many times the people focused on pleasing the missionaries and viewed Christian service "as service of the Mission rather than as the service of Christ."[21]

Allen was also concerned with the problem that with paid positions came covetousness. The people began to desire the higher paid positions because they were generally the places of the most honor.[22] An unhealthy hierarchy of structure developed whereby people vied for positions of power and prestige.

Another weakness was that it was difficult for missionaries to determine how much to pay the people. Allen noted that this conundrum was a serious dilemma. If the rate of pay made the workers comfortable, there was the danger of attracting people who were not very spiritual. If the rate of pay was too little, there would be the danger of starving the workers so that they could not focus on the Lord.[23]

A thirteenth concern for Allen was that the system divided loyalties. Because the stipendiary worker was financially dependent on the Mission, he felt responsible to the Mission or superintending missionary. A sense of responsibility to his congregation was shallow and secondary in nature. Obedience to the directions of the Mission was a must. The support and approval of the Mission was a necessity.[24]

A final concern with the stipendiary system was that it ultimately hindered the spontaneous expansion of the Church. Allen believed that the natural growth of the churches was hindered due to the necessity of a financial foundation for the church to be a church.

> That Churches do not spring up where they live is due to the modern tradition that no Church can be established anywhere without a particular type of cleric especially trained and set apart and paid. It is due to the fact that all our Christians are to-day taught this tradition and are so

bound by it that their hands are tied and their spiritual power is atrophied. This tradition is so powerful that the establishment of new Churches by the scattering of Christians seems to-day almost a revolutionary doctrine.[25]

---

[1] Allen's description and definition of voluntary clergy is as follows: "But we also commonly speak of 'voluntary workers,' meaning men who not only offer their services of their own free will, but also offer their services free of all charge, gratis, as opposed to men who are paid, or receive stipends or allowances, for the work done by them. The term implies nothing derogatory of the service of men who for quite good and sufficient reasons receive stipends. It marks an accidental, not an essential, distinction. It is in this sense that we speak of voluntary clergy. In the first sense of the word we might say that all Christian workers are volunteers, and their service voluntary; but not in the second, the sense in which men habitually use the term as opposed to stipendiary, or paid. Voluntary clergy are men who earn their living by the work of their hands or of their heads in the common market, and serve as clergy without stipend or fee of any kind" (Roland Allen, *The Case for Voluntary Clergy* [London: Eyre and Spottiswoode, 1930], 80-81).

[2] Ibid., 201.

[3] Ibid.

[4] Ibid., 201-02.

[5] Ibid., 26.

[6] Roland Allen, "The Priesthood of the Church," *The Church Quarterly Review* 229 (1933): 234.

[7] Roland Allen, *The Spontaneous Expansion of the Church and the Causes Which Hinder It*, 1st American ed.(Grand Rapids, MI: William B. Eerdmans, 1962), 112.

[8] Ibid., 113.

[9] Ibid., 11.

[10] Allen, *The Case for Voluntary Clergy*, 79.

[11] Ibid., 81.

[12] Ibid., 50.

[13] Ibid., 50, 51.

[14] Even Allen's grandso's words resound with this confusion: "I myself recall a discussion with a school mate about how much people ought to be paid. . . . Granfer, who was also in the room, murmured words to the effect that the Church had a duty to pay its servants properly, but that—*being a priest is not a job. No-one should be paid for being a priest.* My friend and I didn't follow this: it seemed to both of us obvious that being a priest was 'a job'. So Granfer went on: *It is a privilege and a vocation, not a job.* I wasn't at all sure what all these words meant, but Grannie told us not to weary him with questions—and no-one ever argued with Grannie." Hubert J. B. Allen, *Roland Allen*, 122-23.

[15] Roland Allen, "Voluntary Clergy and the Lambeth Conference," *The Church Overseas* (1931): 153.

[16] One example of a major difference was the contemporary practice of the ordination of young people who had not truly experienced life or had time to develop a healthy reputation, but rather received ordination because of their education. Allen had much to say about the discrepancies between the contemporary qualifications and the apostolic qualifications. See Roland Allen, *The Case for Voluntary Clergy*, 41-78.

[17] Allen, *The Case for Voluntary Clergy*, 88.

[18] Ibid., 88-89.

[19] Ibid., 123.

[20] Roland Allen, "Voluntary Service in the Mission Field," *World Dominion* 5 (1927): 136.

[21] Ibid., 137.

[22] Ibid., 138.

[23] Ibid., 139.

[24] Ibid., 141.

[25] Allen, *The Case for Voluntary Clergy*, 129.

Chapter 11
Nonprofessional Missionaries

A close relative to Allen's conception of voluntary clergy was that of nonprofessional missionaries. Though this concept did not receive much attention in his missiology compared to his other thoughts, he did address this issue.[1] After having printed one of Allen's pamphlets entitled "Missionaries Professional and Non-Professional" (1929), the World Dominion Press soon withdrew it from publication. Allen later commented that the pamphlet was withdrawn because a society secretary viewed it as contrary to the policy of the press. Allen felt so strongly about the contents of his writing that he issued it himself, and re-entitled the writing "Non-professional Missionaries."[2]

Allen firmly believed when people dichotomized *missionary work* and *secular work*, they established an unbiblical distinction that the apostle Paul never accepted.[3]

> If we are prepared to believe that every Christian ought to be a missionary, we must also be prepared to admit that every Christian ought to be a missionary *in* his ordinary daily work, all the time, not merely outside it, and part of the time; that "work for the Lord" includes his ordinary daily work, and is not to be treated as something which he can do only when he escapes from the work by which he earns his living.[4]

The nonprofessional missionaries were those who were not sponsored by the mission agencies; they never joined a mission society. These individuals earned their living by their own professions. As they had opportunity to share the gospel, they shared. They believed that they should not receive a salary for evangelism. Allen observed that "they feel that there is something nauseous in offering to others a way of life in Christ except on terms which wholly preclude any possibility that they are seeking anything whatsoever except the other man's salvation."[5] The appellation *missionary* did not apply to these individuals in the technical sense of the word.[6] "They are often spoken of by the professional missionaries as 'men who do a little Christian work in their spare time,' or as 'men who would be all the better if they joined up' [with a mission agency]; but they are doing real missionary work, and it is they who prove that Christians do not only try to give their gospel to others when they have made that work their profession."[7]

Allen contrasted his understanding of the work of the professional missionary with that of the nonprofessional missionary.

> The missionary work of the unofficial missionary is not the same work which a paid professional missionary does. The paid professional missionary leaves the ordinary work of the world and devotes himself to what he calls "religious work;" the non-professional missionary realizes that the ordinary work of the world ought to be done

> religiously, and does it religiously, and calls it "religious work." The professional missionary secularizes all the work which he does not recognize as religious work; the non-professional missionary consecrates all work. The professional missionary exhorts others to consecrate their lives in the common work which he forsakes in order to consecrate his own; the non-professional missionary sets an example of the consecrated life by refusing to forsake his work. The professional missionary preaches by exhortation; the non-professional missionary preaches by example.[8]

Allen's bias was obviously toward nonprofessional missionaries. He was quick to note, however, that just as the apostle Paul did not condemn those who received their livelihood from the ministry, nonprofessional missionaries were not to pass judgment on professional missionaries.[9]

Allen's convictions once again originated with the apostolic pattern. The apostle Paul "did not make any distinction such as we make when we speak of 'missionary work' as peculiarly the work of a special class. In his day the church, as a society, was a missionary society, and each man in the church was a member of a missionary society, and his work, whatever its character, was to be consecrated so that the missionary influence of the church might extend into all departments of life."[10]

Allen further emphasized that professional missionaries were deviating from Pauline practice when they were quick to make a zealous believer a professional missionary. He retold the following story, which illustrated his concern:

> I received the other day a letter in which I was told of a certain bank clerk who had been converted, and of the influence which his life had upon his fellows. My informant added: "Of course now he wants 'to do some work for the Lord.' I tell him that he *is* with a vengeance; but the . . . people have got tight hold of him and have persuaded him to 'join up'—alas!" There is an example of the practice which I described earlier in the chapter. Professional missionaries are naturally inclined to draw any man who shows any care for the souls of his fellows into the professional body. In so acting they are violating the doctrine of St. Paul when he urged men to abide in the calling wherein they were called. "Let each man," he said, "wherein he was called, therein abide with God" (I Cor. 7:24).[11]

Though this Pauline teaching was included in a passage related to marriage, circumcision, and slavery, Allen believed that the teaching had a wider application.

Allen understood that mission societies extracted the leaven from the lump[12] and absorbed too much of the Church's missionary zeal by creating the special class of professional missionaries.[13] The societies were seen as destroying or weakening the "missionary duty of Christian men" by teaching that missionaries were a class apart and their work was not the work of others and by extracting zealous believers from their jobs (i.e., connections with the lost) to do "missionary work."[14] Allen wrote that "it is hard to find anyone who has any missionary zeal who does not take it for granted that he can express it only by supporting one of these societies financially, or by taking service under one of them."[15] He understood that the world would not be reached by professional missionaries and that people needed to be educated about the importance of becoming nonprofessional missionaries.[16]

One reason Allen was biased toward the nonprofessional missionary ideology was because it was a reproducible approach to world evangelization.

> The professional missionary preaches by his example that the way to convert the world is to forsake the common life of men and to live in a special class doing a special work. It is neither possible nor desirable that all Christian men should follow his example. Consequently, if a "missionary" is a man who does that, the exhortation that every Christian should be a missionary becomes absurd: only a few can live the "proper" missionary life. But if a Christian who lives among non-Christians and consciously seeks by his life and conversation to reveal to others the secret of Christ's grace is a missionary, then indeed every Christian ought to be a missionary and do missionary work. Thus the example of the professional missionary, as

> such, is not an example for all; whilst the example of the non-professional missionary is an example for all—an example of universal application.[17]

It is this understanding of universal application that connected nonprofessional missionaries with Allen's concept of spontaneous expansion.

Allen's solution to the Church needing more nonprofessional missionaries was based on changing the contemporary perspective. He encouraged his readers to place emphasis on the necessity of nonprofessional missionaries.

> I suggest that the first step is to find men and women who have a strong and deep missionary spirit and to persuade them that the highest and best missionary work that they can do is to go out into the mission field as "unofficial missionaries," refusing to join themselves officially to the professional missionary body. They should go into government service, into the offices of the great trading houses, into the farming community, into the society of the great cities and towns of non-Christian lands with this deliberate purpose—to show that it is possible for a man, or a woman, to be in the fullest sense "in" that life and yet to be a missionary, to prove to the foreign community and to the native people amongst whom they dwell, that it is possible, and so to leaven the whole lump.[18]

Though this changing of perspective seemed like a fairly simple task, we must remember that in Allen's day (as well as today) the concept of a professional missionary was a deeply entrenched ideology. The changing of a traditional paradigm would not happen overnight. Allen understood that the change would not be immediate. He did, however, offer some more guidance on how to change the perspective.

The Church needed a different assumption. Instead of assuming that a zealous believer would automatically enter into the professional society, the Church should assume that the believer would take on a regular vocation.

> The difficulty is that now, when any young man or woman is moved by the Holy Ghost to take thought for the souls of the heathen, everyone conspires to drive him into the position of a professional missionary, and they do it in the most powerful way, by simply taking it for granted. Here is a man who cares for the souls of non-Christian folk; of course he is going to be a missionary, and by "a missionary" is meant a professional missionary. The power of that tacit assumption is incalculably weighty. It ought to become natural for a man who cares for the souls of non-Christians to be asked what sort of a job he is looking for, and where, and the assumption behind the question should be the assumption that he is probably looking for a post under government or on a farm or in a trading corporation, an assumption only to be avoided by

> the assertion that he is proposing to apply to a missionary society for a post as a professional missionary.[19]

Though the notion of nonprofessional missionaries did not receive a great deal of attention in Allen's published writings, it was an important part of his understanding of what was needed for the multiplication of disciples, leaders, and churches. His convictions grew out of a theology of work that did not know a secular-sacred dichotomy. Allen believed that Western missionaries should not import their tradition of financial support onto the new believers and churches. He recognized that in pioneer areas the Church had the opportunity to begin something new, avoiding some of the problematic issues of the West.

---

[1] Allen's grandson, Hubert J. B. Allen, thought this concept to be so noteworthy that he entitled the tenth chapter of his book "Non-Professional Missionaries." See Hubert J. B. Allen, *Roland Allen: Pioneer, Priest, and Prophet* (Cincinnati, OH: Forward Movement Publications; Grand Rapids, MI: William B. Eerdmans, 1995), 117-27.

[2] Hubert J. B. Allen, *Roland Allen*, 120. Aside from the preface, the entire work was later reprinted in David M. Paton's collection, *The Ministry of the Spirit: Selected Writings of Roland Allen.* Also, the majority of the work can be found in two articles published by the World Dominion Press in 1928: "The Need for Non-professional Missionaries," *World Dominion* 5 (1928): 195-201; and "The Work of Non-professional Missionaries," *World Dominion* 5 (1928): 298-304. Apart from Hubert J. B. Allen's comments as noted above, it is still not clear why World Dominion originally published the majority of Allen's work in two articles and then in pamphlet form before withdrawing it.

[3] Hubert J. B. Allen, *Roland Allen*, 121; Roland Allen, "Non-professional Missionaries," in *The Ministry of the Spirit: Selected Writings of Roland Allen*,

American ed., ed. David M. Paton (Grand Rapids, MI: William B. Eerdmans, 1960), 83.

[4] Roland Allen, "Non-professional Missionaries," 81-82. Allen was not one who believed that just any task or work could be labeled as evangelism, but rather that everything the individual did was for the purpose of communicating the gospel to the lost. For example, someone worked as a farmer for the purpose of taking the gospel to others. A person could not be a missionary without being evangelistic. Allen wrote: "By a 'missionary of the gospel' I understand a man who having found the secret of life in Christ is eager to impart it to others. The gospel is for him the only way of life; there can be no other: men who do not share his secret are living in darkness and perishing in their ignorance: that is the difference between a missionary of the gospel and a lecturer on comparative religion. A missionary is therefore an evangelist"
(Ibid., 65).

[5] Ibid., 74.

[6] Ibid., 74, 75.

[7] Ibid., 75.

[8] Ibid., 82.

[9] Ibid., 74.

[10] Ibid., 83.

[11] Ibid., 80-81.

[12] Ibid., 81.

[13] Ibid., 77.

[14] Ibid., 83.

[15] Ibid., 77.

[16] Ibid., 81.

[17] Ibid., 82.

[18] Ibid., 78.

[19] Ibid., 79.

Conclusion

If asked to describe Allen's missiology in the briefest of terms, we could respond with "spontaneous expansion." All of his missiological views related to this concept in some fashion. Certain concepts, such as native education, voluntary clergy, and nonprofessional missionaries were important to the overall understanding of spontaneous expansion, but were secondary in nature. They derived themselves out of a context whereby a proper biblical and theological foundation had been established, the missionary's role was clearly understood, and a healthy understanding of indigenous churches was present. If any of the various components as discussed in this book—theology, the place of the missionary, indigenous churches, native education, voluntary clergy, or nonprofessional missionaries—hindered spontaneous expansion, Allen would have been the first to discard that component.

Allen viewed the spontaneous expansion of the Church as something without any restraints placed on the Church's natural instinct. He understood that "spontaneous expansion must be free: it cannot be under our control; and consequently it is utterly vain to say, as I constantly hear men say, that we desire to see spontaneous expansion, and yet must maintain our control. If we want to see spontaneous expansion we must establish native churches free from our control."[1] Allen compared men who believed in spontaneous expansion but were unwilling to abandon control to "children who will not go into the dark while yet they declare that they are not afraid, or like women who are not happy without their mascot while they say that they do not believe in luck."[2]

Allen understood, however, the natural fear that missionaries had when it came to spontaneous expansion. In fact, Allen himself had a great fear of the thought of the Church expanding without any Western control. He even referred to spontaneous expansion as "the terror of missionaries."[3] He sympathized with many of his colleagues when he stated:

> When I think of a Native Church fully equipped with spiritual authority spontaneously expanding in Africa, or in China, or in India, without any control which we could *enforce,* either by threats of withdrawal of grants of money, or by the exercise of a governmental authority which we keep in our own hands, I confess that I tremble. . . . Am I not right in saying that spontaneous expansion viewed from the far distance as something to be hoped for in many years to come is an attractive vision; but that when we come close to it, and view it as something which we ought to expect to-day, it appears a horrible monster?[4]

The thought of the Church in a particular region growing without any oversight from more mature believers was a paralyzing thought. Allen realized that if spontaneous expansion occurred at least five results were to be expected. First, the local church members would lead such lifestyles that others would desire to become a part of the church. Second, church members of their own free will would begin to persuade others to join the church. Next, church members who traveled throughout the country for business or pleasure would begin to share the gospel with others who would soon desire to establish a church where they lived. Closely related to this latter statement is the idea that churches would begin to form in new places without any direction from the mission agency. Finally, the new churches that were established would repeat these same processes of spontaneous expansion.[5]

Allen's fear of spontaneous expansion was because these five natural results could not be organized, directed, or controlled by a mission agency. He understood that there was no way to oversee the speech and conduct of the believers in their homes, marketplaces, or while they were visiting friends and relatives. It was impossible for an agency to control the establishment of new churches under such circumstances.[6] Despite his fears, he believed that spontaneous expansion was the biblical pattern and, therefore, turned to the Scriptures to find solace for his concerns.[7]

Within the apostolic pattern, he found the proper perspective for overcoming the fear that hindered the spontaneous expansion of the Church. Missionaries were to manifest a proper faith in the Bridegroom, instead of focusing on the imperfections and immaturity of the Bride. In essence, the missionaries were to yield control to the Spirit who indwelled the new believers. Examining the Pauline pattern, Allen wrote:

> We are concentrating our attention upon the weakness of man, we are thinking wholly of the weakness of our converts. Is that quite right? I turn to the New Testament and I read of the terrible failings of those little groups of Christians living in heathen cities surrounded by every insidious form of heathen immorality and heathen thought, and I find the Apostle writing to them, not as if he had any faith in them, or in their strength or character, or in their natural virtue, but in quite other terms, of his faith that Christ will work in them, that Christ has called them, that Christ will enlighten them, that Christ will save them. . . . Again I turn to the New Testament, and I find the Apostle of the Gentiles relying not upon his authority, his government, his control but upon something very different. He trusts in God in Christ to meet the obvious and very present dangers. He does not shut his eyes to the dangers, the falls, the ignorance, the weakness of his converts, but that does not prevent him from establishing his Churches in this freedom, or from looking upon spontaneous expansion as something present and admirable.[8]

It is in this lack of control that the reader finds a paradox in Allen's thinking. In order for the missionaries to be in control of what the Scriptures prescribe as proper missionary functions, they must be out of control. Surrender to the Lord's oversight of His congregation is a must. Without this faith, missionaries find themselves kicking against the goads. In the conclusion of *The Spontaneous Expansion of the Church*, Allen admonished his readers to manifest a healthy missionary faith:

> What is necessary is faith. What is needed is the kind of faith which, uniting a man to Christ, sets him on fire. Such a man can believe that others finding Christ will be set on fire also. Such a man can see that there is no need of money to fill a continent with the knowledge of Christ. Such a man can see that all that is required to consolidate and establish that expansion is the simple application of the simple organization of the Church. It is to men who know that faith, who see that vision, that I appeal. Let them judge what I have written.[9]

Despite the lengthy discussion of the components of Allen's missiology as noted within this book, his concept of spontaneous expansion is fairly simple. In light of his missiology, I have developed what I refer to as the Roland Allen Equation for the Spontaneous Expansion of the Church. I realize that there are at least two possible weaknesses with displaying Allen's views as a linear equation.

First, there is the accusation of being too reductionistic. It is my hope that within the context of this book, this accusation will be leveled. When readers examine the breadth and depth of Allen's missiology, they will hopefully understand that I have not attempted to deconstruct Allen to a point that is more basic than the simplicity of his understanding of spontaneous expansion.

The second possible accusation of compiling the equation is that Allen never offered a formula and, therefore, no contemporary scholar should attempt to place his views in separate vacuums. Allen never dichotomized his views to the point whereby they could be neatly separated from one another. His thoughts ranging from his theology to his missiology were all interwoven and focused on a particular result: spontaneous expansion of the Church.

The reason that I have attempted to develop an equation that displays Allen's understanding of spontaneous expansion is primarily for pedagogical matters. Allen was a prolific writer. It takes some time for someone to chart the waters of the literature that contain his missiology. The church needs a visual portraying Allen's understanding of spontaneous expansion for the purpose of easily grasping his thought. By portraying his thoughts as a formula, I have no desire to attempt to convey the belief that if someone adds this component to that component the result will be spontaneous expansion. Allen himself never made that type of statement.

Allen's views called for a radical paradigm shift, not a step-by-step process for church growth. This shift reverted to a biblical simplicity of an apostolic pattern, a pattern that consisted of simple missionary belief, practice, and church organization. The following quote showed the radical nature of the necessary paradigm shift.

> Thus there can be no place for the man who would practise Pauline principles in the modern missions. He cannot follow their policies, he cannot understand their treaties, he cannot assist in the establishment and expansion of their peculiar codes of morals, or of religious practices. He would be rejected at once by any mission board. . . . There is no possible answer to the man who asks how to apply Pauline principles to modern mission stations. There is no possible escape from the charge of madness for anyone who would practise them. There is no half-way house. It is not in the external superficial appearances that the difference between us and St. Paul lies, but in the Spirit of freedom which that Spirit induced. That is the fundamental distinction.[10]

When we study Allen, we encounter another missiological paradox. On the one hand, the spontaneous expansion is very simple and is appropriate for any given context.

> The spontaneous expansion of the Church reduced to its elements is a very simple thing. It asks for no elaborate organization, no large finances, no great numbers of paid missionaries. In its beginning it may be the work of one man, and that a man neither learned in the things of this world, nor rich in the wealth of this world. The organization of a little church on the apostolic model is also extremely simple, and the most illiterate converts can

use it, and the poorest are sufficiently wealthy to maintain it. Only as it grows and spreads through large provinces and countries do any complex questions arise, and they arise only as a church composed of many little churches is able to produce leaders prepared to handle them by experience learned in the smaller things.[11]

On the other hand, as noted in a previous quote above, spontaneous expansion requires a radical and difficult paradigm shift. When working within the established missional paradigm, the paradox is ever present. The paradox can only be avoided, and the simplicity of spontaneous expansion grasped and applied, apart from any reins of an established system like Allen faced in his day.

The Roland Allen Equation for the Spontaneous Expansion of the Church, in essence, consists of three components. Allen's views concerning indigenous churches and the Holy Spirit must be realized and accepted. And, missionary faith that is opposed to devolution must be present. As the equation shows, when the concept of indigenous churches is united with the proper understanding of the Holy Spirit and missionary faith is present, the result is the spontaneous expansion of the Church (see Figure 3).

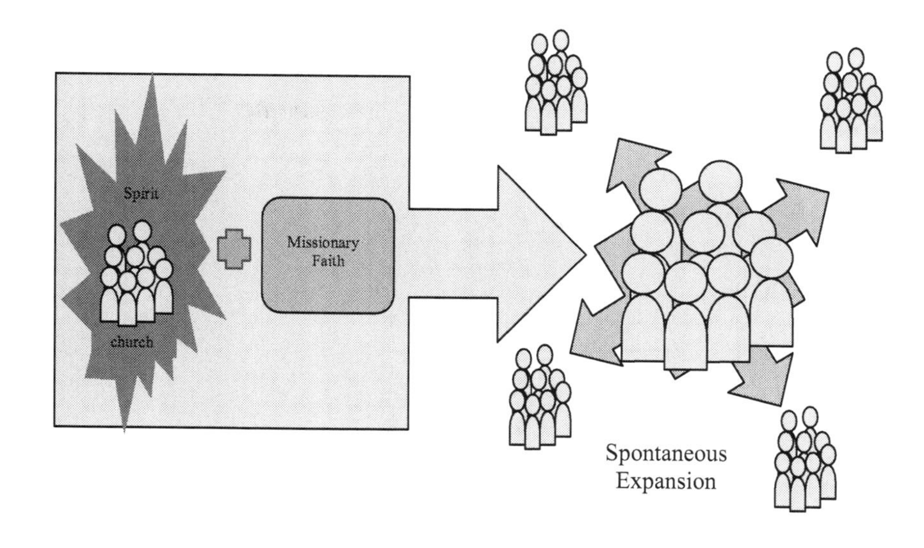

Figure 3. The Roland Allen Equation for the Spontaneous Expansion of the Church

---

[1] Roland Allen, *The Spontaneous Expansion of the Church and the Causes Which Hinder It*, 1st American ed. (Grand Rapids, MI: William B. Eerdmans, 1962), 5.

[2] Roland Allen, "Spontaneous Expansion: The Terror of Missionaries," *World Dominion* 4 (1926): 223.

[3] Ibid.

[4] Ibid., 221.

[5] Ibid., 219-20.

[6] Ibid., 220.

[7] This concept of fear was the hindrance to spontaneous expansion. In Allen's writings, he stated that "the greatest of all hindrances to the immediate appearance of a wide spreading spontaneous expansion is this unbelief on our part which fears spontaneous expansion; for that impresses upon all men a sense that it is something at once terrible and impossible" (Ibid., 223).

[8] Ibid., 221-22.

[9] Allen, *The Spontaneous Expansion of the Church*, 157.

[10] Roland Allen, "The Application of Pauline Principles to Modern Missions," *World Dominion* 11 (1933): 356, 357.

[11] Allen, *The Spontaneous Expansion of the Church*, 156.

Bibliography

Books by Roland Allen

__________. *Missionary Methods*: St. Paul's or Ours? London: Robert Scott, 1912. Reprint, London: World Dominion Press, 1930, 1949, 1956. Reprint, Grand Rapids, MI: William B. Eerdmans, 1962, 1998.

__________. *Missionary Principles*. London: Robert Scott, 1913. Reprint, *Essential Missionary Principles*. New York: Fleming H. Revell Company, 1913.

__________. *Pentecost, and the World: The Revelation of the Holy Spirit in the "Acts of the Apostles."* London: Oxford University Press, 1917.

__________. *Educational Principles and Missionary Methods: The Application of Educational Principles to Missionary Evangelism*. London: Robert Scott, 1919.

__________. *Voluntary Clergy*. London: S.P.C.K., 1923.

__________. *The Spontaneous Expansion of the Church and the Causes Which Hinder It*. London: World Dominion Press, 1927. Re-issued, 1949 and 1956. London: World Dominion Press, 1960.

__________. *Voluntary Clergy Overseas*: *An Answer to the Fifth World Call*. Beaconsfield: privately printed, 1928.

__________. *S. J. W. Clark: A Vision of Foreign Missions*. London: World Dominion Press, 1937.

__________. *The Case for Voluntary Clergy*. London: Eyre and Spottiswoode, 1940.

__________.*The Ministry of the Spirit—Selected Writings of Roland Allen*. Edited by David M. Paton and Charles H. Long. Grand Rapids, MI: William B. Eerdmans; Cincinnati, OH: Forward Movement Publications, 1983.

__________.*The Compulsion of the Spirit—A Roland Allen Reader.* Edited by David Paton and Charles H. Long. Grand Rapids, MI: William B. Eerdmans; Cincinnati, OH: Forward Movement Publications, 1983.

Booklets and Pamphlets by Roland Allen

Allen, Roland. *Education in the Native Church*. London: World Dominion Press, 1926.

__________.*Devolution and its Real Significance*. London: World Dominion Press, 1927.

__________.*Le Zoute: A Critical Review of 'The Christian Mission in Africa.'* London: World Dominion Press, 1927.

__________.*The Establishment of the Church in the Mission Field: A Critical Dialogue*. London: World Dominion Press, 1927.

__________.*Jerusalem: A Critical Review of 'The World Mission of Christianity.'* London: World Dominion Press, 1928.

__________.*Non-Professional Missionaries.* Beaconsfield: privately printed, 1929.

__________.*The 'Nevius Method' in Korea.* London: World Dominion Press, 1930.

__________.*Mission Activities Considered in Relation to the Manifestation of the Spirit.* N.p., n.d. 2nd ed. World Dominion Press, 1930.

__________.*The Place of 'Faith' in Missionary Evangelism.* London: World Dominion Press, 1930.

__________.*Discussion on Mission Education.* London: World Dominion Press, 1931.

Articles by Roland Allen

Allen, Roland. "Of Some of the Causes Which Led to the Preservation of the Foreign Legations in Peking." *The Cornhill* (1900): 754-76

__________. "Of Some of the Conclusions Which May be Drawn from the Siege of the Foreign Legations in Pekin." *The Cornhill* (1901): 202-12.

__________. "The Christian Education of Native Churches." *Church Missionary Review* (1918): 398-405.

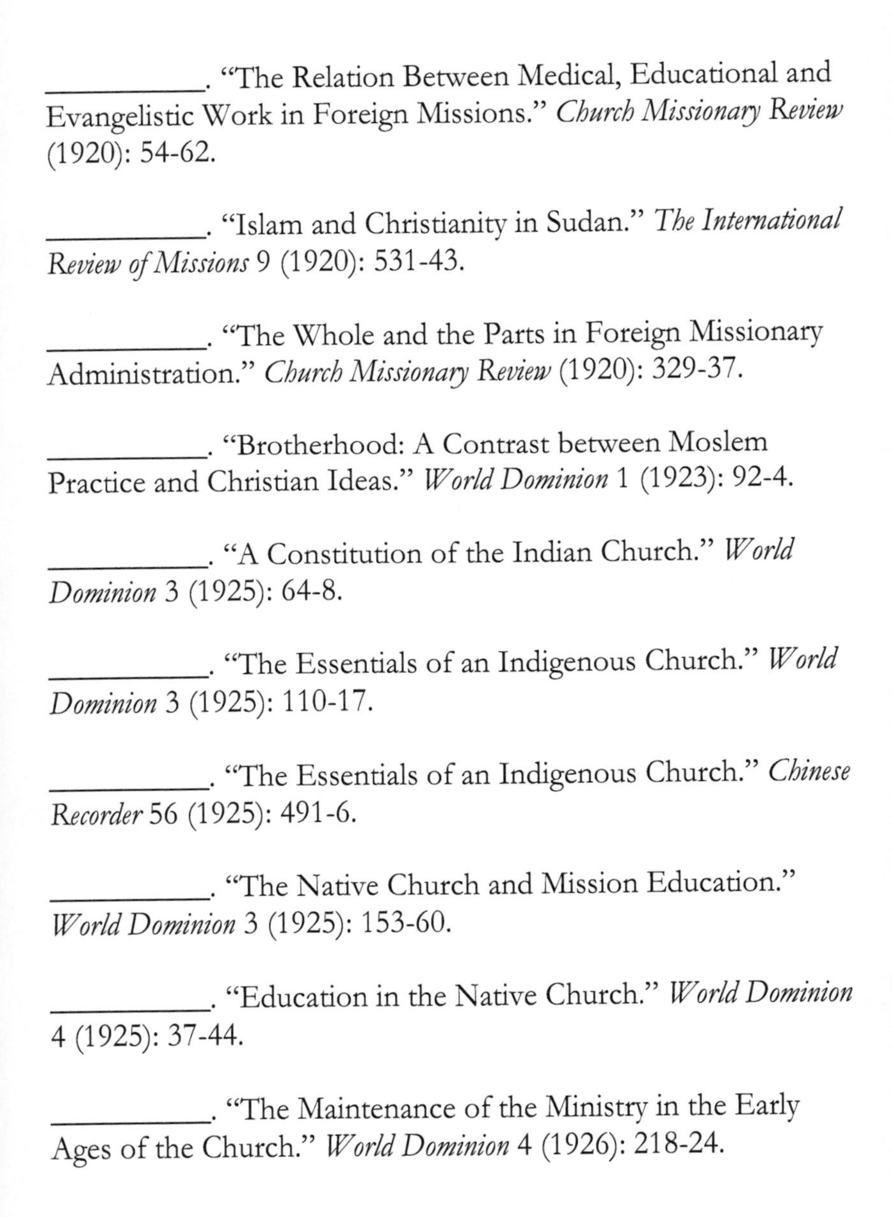

__________. “The Relation Between Medical, Educational and Evangelistic Work in Foreign Missions.” *Church Missionary Review* (1920): 54-62.

__________. “Islam and Christianity in Sudan.” *The International Review of Missions* 9 (1920): 531-43.

__________. “The Whole and the Parts in Foreign Missionary Administration.” *Church Missionary Review* (1920): 329-37.

__________. “Brotherhood: A Contrast between Moslem Practice and Christian Ideas.” *World Dominion* 1 (1923): 92-4.

__________. “A Constitution of the Indian Church.” *World Dominion* 3 (1925): 64-8.

__________. “The Essentials of an Indigenous Church.” *World Dominion* 3 (1925): 110-17.

__________. “The Essentials of an Indigenous Church.” *Chinese Recorder* 56 (1925): 491-6.

__________. “The Native Church and Mission Education.” *World Dominion* 3 (1925): 153-60.

__________. “Education in the Native Church.” *World Dominion* 4 (1925): 37-44.

__________. “The Maintenance of the Ministry in the Early Ages of the Church.” *World Dominion* 4 (1926): 218-24.

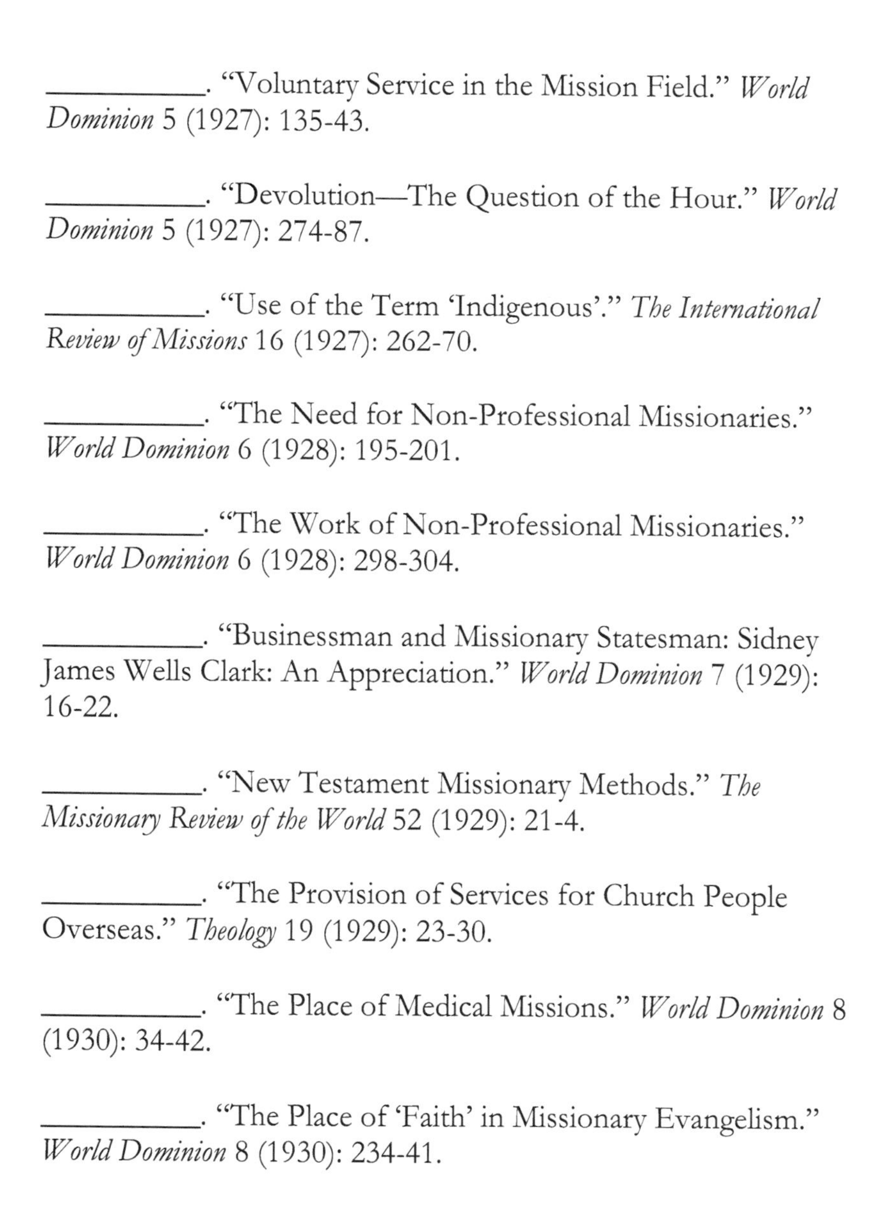

__________. "Voluntary Service in the Mission Field." *World Dominion* 5 (1927): 135-43.

__________. "Devolution—The Question of the Hour." *World Dominion* 5 (1927): 274-87.

__________. "Use of the Term 'Indigenous'." *The International Review of Missions* 16 (1927): 262-70.

__________. "The Need for Non-Professional Missionaries." *World Dominion* 6 (1928): 195-201.

__________. "The Work of Non-Professional Missionaries." *World Dominion* 6 (1928): 298-304.

__________. "Businessman and Missionary Statesman: Sidney James Wells Clark: An Appreciation." *World Dominion* 7 (1929): 16-22.

__________. "New Testament Missionary Methods." *The Missionary Review of the World* 52 (1929): 21-4.

__________. "The Provision of Services for Church People Overseas." *Theology* 19 (1929): 23-30.

__________. "The Place of Medical Missions." *World Dominion* 8 (1930): 34-42.

__________. "The Place of 'Faith' in Missionary Evangelism." *World Dominion* 8 (1930): 234-41.

__________. "The Chinese Government and Mission Schools." *World Dominion* 9 (1931): 25-30.

__________. "Voluntary Clergy and the Lambeth Conference." *The Church Overseas* (1931): 145-53.

__________. "The 'Nevius Method' in Korea." *World Dominion* 9 (1931): 252-58.

__________. "The Priesthood of the Church." *The Church Quarterly Review* 116 (1933): 234-44.

__________. "The Application of Pauline Principles to Modern Missions." *World Dominion* 11 (1933): 352-57.

Books and Articles about Roland Allen

Allen, Hubert J.B. *Roland Allen: Pioneer, Priest and Prophet.* Cincinnati, OH: Forward Movement Publications; Grand Rapids, MI: William B. Eerdmans, 1995.

Allen, Priscilla M. "Roland Allen: A Prophet for this Age." *The Living Church* (April 20, 1986): 9-11.

Boer, H.R. "Roland Allen—Voice in the Wilderness." *World Dominion* 32 (1954): 224-31.

__________. "Roland Allen, the Holy Spirit, and Missions." *World Dominion* 33 (1955): 297-303.

Branner, John E. "Roland Allen: Pioneer in a Spirit-Centered Theology of Mission." *Missiology* 5 (1977): 175-84.

Cochrane, Thomas. "Roland Allen." *World Dominion* 26 (1948): 66.

Long, Charles H., and Ann Rowthorn. "The Legacy of Roland Allen." *International Bulletin of Missionary Research* 13 (1989): 65-68.

Paton, David Macdonald, "The Relevance of Roland Allen." In *Part-time Priests*, ed. Robin Denniston. London: Skeffington, 1960.

__________. "Three Prophets: F.D. Maurice, H.H. Kelly, Roland Allen." *Frontier* 3 (August 1960): n.p.

__________, ed. "Roland Allen—A Biographical and Theological Essay." In *Reform of the Ministry: A Study in the Work of Roland Allen.* London: Lutterworth Press, 1968.

Payne, J.D. "The Legacy of Roland Allen" *Churchman* 117 (2003): 315-328.

__________. "Missiology of Roland Allen" *The Journal of the American Society for Church Growth* 15 (2004): 45-118.

__________. "Roland Allen." In *The Encyclopedia of Christian Literature,* Vol 1, eds. George Thomas Kurian and James D. Smith III. U.K.: The Scarecrow Press, Inc. (2010): 171-173.

__________. "'Messing Up' Missionary Endeavors: Celebrating Roland Allen's *Missionary Methods*" *Evangelical Missions Quarterly* 48, No. 1 (January 2012): 6-7.

Porter, H. Boone, Jr. "Roland Allen: Prophet and Priest." *The Living Church* (May 19, 1963): 14-15, 29.

Sanderson, David. "Roland Allen: A Prophet for a 'Decade of Evangelism'." *Modern Churchman* 34 (1993): 13-19.

Talltort, A. *Sacrament and Growth: A Study of the Sacramental Dimension of Expansion in the Life of the Local Church, as Reflected in the Theology of Roland Allen*. Uppsala: n.p., 1989.

Wood, C. "The Minyerri Vision: Roland Allen in Australia." In *Reshaping Ministry: Essays in Memory of Wesley Frensdorff*, ed. Josephine Borgeson and Lynne Wilson. Arvada, CO: Jethro Publishers, 1990.

Dissertations and Thesis about Roland Allen

Branner, John K. "Roland Allen, Donald McGavran and Church Growth." Th.M. thesis, Fuller Theological Seminary, 1975.

Burkhalter, William Nolan. "A Comparative Analysis of the Missiologies of Roland Allen and Donald Anderson McGavran." Ph.D. diss., The Southern Baptist Theological Seminary, 1984.

Cheruvil, Joseph. "Roland Allen's Missionary Insights: Their Relevance to a North Indian Context." Ph.D. diss., Katholieke Universiteit Leuven, 1993.

Payne, Jervis D. "An Evaluation of the Systems Approach to North American Church Multiplication Movements of Robert E. Logan in Light of the Missiology of Roland Allen," Ph.D. diss., The Southern Baptist Theological Seminary, 2001.

Schnackenbeg, Gerald, L. "An Examination of Roland Allen's Missiology with Suggestions for Appropriation of Some of His Principles in the Anglican Church Among the Bantu People of Malawi." M.A.R. thesis, Lliff School of Theology, 1987.

Sims, John Ronald. "Financial Self-Support and Sharing among the Churches Worldwide: A Historical and Missiological Study." D.Miss. diss., Fuller Theological Seminary, 1989.

Tang, Li. "Rediscovering Roland Allen: A Survey of His Theology Concerning the Christian World Mission." M.A.R. thesis, Emmanuel School of Religion, 1991.

Thompson, Michael Don. "The Holy Spirit and Human Instrumentality in the Training of New Converts: An Evaluation of the Missiological Thought of Roland Allen." Ph.D. diss., Golden Gate Baptist Theological Seminary, 1989.

Wulf, Craig M. "The Missiology of Roland Allen." M.Div. thesis, Concordia Theological Seminary, 1980.

Printed in Great Britain
by Amazon